Contents

IMPROVING READING

A TEACHER'S GUIDE
TO
PEER-TUTORING

Frank Merrett

David Fulton Publishers

London

David Fulton Publishers Ltd
2 Barbon Close, London WC1N 3JX

First published in Great Britain by
David Fulton Publishers 1994

Note: The right of Frank Merrett to be identified as the author of this work has
been asserted by him in accordance with the Copyright, Designs and Patents
Act 1988.

British Library Cataloguing in Publication Data

A catalogue record for this book is available from the British Library

ISBN 1-85346-326-4

Typeset by the author
Printed in Great Britain by BPC Books and Journals, Exeter

Preface

One of the major problems facing secondary education in England and Wales today is that many of the children entering our high schools do so with inadequate reading skills. The proportion of such children is not known with any degree of accuracy but from information received from concerned teachers it is as high as 25% in some areas. Most teachers in secondary schools do not realise that such a problem exists. They assume that because pupils come to them through the primary system they must be able to read since teaching their pupils to read is the chief function of primary schools. Some have been known to express the view that the reading skills of their pupils are, in any case, no concern of theirs since they are teachers of specialist subjects.

Generally speaking, their professional training gives secondary school teachers no information about how children learn to read, about how to measure reading skills, about the importance of issues like readability, size of print and so on. Frequently, when pupils enter secondary school they are given texts to read about the specialist subjects they are to study without anyone having given thought to matching the level of difficulty of the text with the reading skills of the children. Children are given text books in history, physics, geography and, indeed, in almost any subject which are basically too difficult for a high proportion of them to read quickly and with understanding. The result is that these pupils do not comprehend the material they have been asked to master and when asked questions on it are not able to respond adequately. Their written responses are likely to be even less acceptable to teachers than their oral answers as poor readers find difficulty also with writing. Where this mismatch occurs pupils begin to fail from the very first day.

A survey carried out recently in which teachers reported on the behaviour of their pupils showed that high on their list of complaints was idleness and slowness, particularly among the older pupils. Before teachers begin to deplore the increasing number of disaffected pupils in the upper forms of our secondary schools perhaps they should address the problem outlined above. There are some teachers in secondary schools who recognize the problem for what it is and are endeavouring to do something constructive about it. They are mainly those employed as support teachers or remedial teachers who have the necessary concern and knowledge but most of them lack the facilities and support that are essential.

The purpose of this book is to explore the means that teachers might employ to seek a solution to this very difficult and largely unrecognised problem. After an introduction outlining the need for literacy, the idea of using other children as tutors is introduced, elaborated and justified. The next four chapters outline some of the procedures which have been developed to bring about the accelerated progress in reading skill which is necessary for pupils who have fallen behind. These include shared reading or relaxed reading, paired reading and the very powerful pause, prompt and praise procedures.

Chapters 8, 9 and 10 give details of the research underlying these approaches and references to all the papers and books cited are listed alphabetically in the first part of Chapter 12. The section about research has been separated from the descriptions of the different approaches as some readers will not be interested in or feel the need for this sort of detailed information. Chapter 11 is concerned with the problem of evaluating the outcomes of peer-tutoring projects. Setting up a project takes courage and perseverance because there are many obstacles to be overcome. A good evaluation of positive outcomes can be influential in persuading colleagues and others in authority and in creating allies to further the good work. Chapter 12 gives some more valuable references to books on tutoring schemes, recommended series of books, books of general interest for children, reading tests, associations concerned with progress in reading and other sources of information about peer-tutoring. The hope is that this information, which includes reports on some programmes which are already established and producing good results, will enthuse other teachers and be of assistance in setting up further successful peer-tutoring schemes in schools.

CHAPTER ONE

Introduction

The *Handbook of Suggestions for Teachers* published in 1937 by the Ministry of Education suggested that the primary school stage provided the opportunity for acquiring the 'three Rs', the tools of learning, whilst the secondary stage gave the opportunity for exercising those skills in furthering education and developing the person. Educational ideas and practice have moved far since those days but, nevertheless, the basic notion is as true today as it was then and the key to further education is undoubtedly the skill of reading.

No-one would dispute the fact that the ability to read is of the utmost importance for everyone. Indeed, it is essential for successful living in modern society. At the very least every citizen needs to be able to read a warning sign, a newspaper (even if only the advertisements or the television programmes in the local free newspaper), a D.I.Y. manual, a recipe book, an application form, a tax return, an advertisement and so on. Almost all occupations require some degree of skill in interpreting and understanding the printed word. One of the conclusions of the Bullock Committee (D.E.S., 1975) was that,

> The level of reading skill required for participation in the affairs of modern society is far above that implied in earlier definitions of literacy. (p. 516)

Adults who cannot read have a much reduced self-image and a feeling that, somehow, they are inadequate. The success of the Adult Literacy Programme in Britain in recent years bears witness to this fact. Adults who cannot read adopt all manner of ploys to avoid the consequences of their inability and to hide their lack of skill. Given the opportunity to learn under sympathetic and skilled guidance large numbers give up time and make the effort to retrieve the situation. I remember being told by a district superviser of the Adult Literacy

Programme of a middle-aged man who expressed great regret that he was not able to carry out simple calculations. It was established that he had no practical need for such skills. His job did not require him to be able to calculate yet he felt inadequate and believed that he ought to be able to do this. The urge to learn the skill was so great that he was prepared to devote time to it, even at this late stage. Clearly, it is better if people learn to cope adequately with the 'three Rs' at the time when most others do, that is, at school. If they do not the consequences for them and for their job prospects can be severe.

Above all the ability to read is absolutely essential for success in secondary and any higher form of education. At university level the question about a person's academic interests is put by asking, 'What are you reading?'. It is assumed that knowledge and understanding are gained principally through reading. One of the most important recent innovations in education has been the development of distance learning and clearly this would be impossible if the students could not read well and quickly. Increasingly, courses in higher and further education are being delivered at a distance and in all such distance learning courses the major part of the new information comes through reading, supplemented by audio and video tapes, tutorials, and weekend and Summer schools. The very successful Open University has been organised on these lines for many years and provides a model for other distance learning courses. I have a number of degrees, diplomas and fellowships all of which, except my original teacher training qualification and my M.A., were acquired as an external or part-time student of a university. All of these academic qualifications were dependent upon the ability to work alone and to learn through reading.

At the moment there is great controversy about the best method for teaching reading and a lot of heart searching as to if or why standards of literacy are falling. Nearly twenty years ago the compilers of *A Language for Life* (The Bullock Report, D.E.S., 1975) concluded that, "there is no one method, medium, approach, device or philosophy that holds the key to the process of learning to read" (p. 77). In another section this important report described the basic demands of reading in these words,

What are these demands? This question is best answered in terms of three basic objectives, simple enough on paper but far from simple in the execution:

(a) the pupil should be able to cope with the reading required in each area of the curriculum;

(b) he should acquire a level of competence which will enable him to meet his needs as an adult in society when he leaves school;

(c) he should regard reading as a source of pleasure and personal development which will continue to be a rewarding activity throughout life. (p. 115)

One of the most important facts underlined in the Bullock Report is that reading is a developmental process involving the mastery of a hierarchy of increasingly complex, interrelated skills from pre-school to university. Stress is laid on the fact that in order to meet these demands most children require explicit instruction from expert teachers throughout their school careers. The Report denies the well-established fallacy that the teaching of reading is the sole responsibility of teachers of infants or of older, backward pupils and revives the maxim that 'every teacher is, or should be, a teacher of reading'.

The Bullock Report made the point that delay in making even a modest start in reading beyond the age of seven puts the child at educational risk, not merely because a good deal of learning depends on the ability to read, but because poor readers are less likely to receive skilled attention the older they become. The Report drew attention to the fact that children behind at seven drop even further behind at eleven, and the number of children who continue to need extra help at secondary level is considerable. Children who read well at seven will probably be reading a great deal and their skills grow rapidly through practice. Poor readers, on the other hand, receive less and less practice and even if they were to make 'normal' progress they would still remain far behind the rest. They need to make accelerated progress in order to reach normality in reading.

There are many contributory causes for failure to make progress in reading. These include the home environment, the economic environment, sensory defects, limited mental ability, anxiety, depression and so on. There is a close association between retardation in reading and emotional disorders. Poor readers are almost four times as likely as other children to show signs of maladjustment in school. There is not much encouraging evidence on the effectiveness of 'remedial' education. In chapter 18 of the Bullock Report it was suggested that certain factors are essential if success is to be broad and lasting.

Firstly, each child's particular difficulties must be related to his whole linguistic development. The methods employed with readers who are making slow progress are not intrinsically different from those employed in any successful teaching but the essence is that more time and resources should go to adapting the methods to individual needs and difficulties.

Secondly, warm relationships need to be created between teachers and pupils so that they are encouraged to learn through the stimulus of success. The suggestion is that sound teaching should be applied to ensure that failure is replaced by a sense of achievement and that confidence and self-esteem are increased. It is stressed that this is a task not for the inexpert or inexperienced but rather for those who combine a high level of teaching skill with an understanding of the child's emotional and developmental needs.

Thirdly, remedial reading should be linked to the rest of a child's learning whenever possible. The point is made that in many cases children who receive extra help enjoy fewer opportunities to achieve success in other activities such as crafts, art, drama and music. Prolonged emphasis on remedial work at the expense of other parts of the curriculum may be self-defeating.

Fourthly, every attempt should be made to involve parents and help them to understand their children's difficulties. It has sometimes been assumed, quite wrongly, that parents are not concerned about their children's lack of progress in reading. The Report draws attention to the fact that if the interest of the parents is capitalised upon they can play a vitally constructive part in helping their own children.

It is with the first of the demands listed on pages 2 and 3, i.e. functional reading, that this book is mainly concerned. Recent reports from Her Majesty's Inspectorate have indicated that there is a serious disparity between the reading ability of a proportion of children entering the secondary stage of education and the kind of reading material contained in the texts used by teachers in the early years of secondary schooling. Primary head teachers will often assert that all children leaving their schools are able to read. However, if one goes to the local secondary school and asks the teachers there about the functional reading levels of their entrants, one hears a different story. In many secondary schools the number assessed as unable to read adequately for the purposes of Year 7 work can be anything up to 30%. It is plain that children who are unable to cope with simple texts will begin to fail from the very start of their secondary schooling.

Most specialist teachers in secondary schools will not be conversant with concepts such as readability and will assume that the children coming to them at age 11 will be able to read well enough to cope. This mismatch between expectation and fact will have a profound effect on the success of many pupils and it is not surprising that many of them caught in this trap find little satisfaction in their school work. As a result, many develop patterns of behaviour that teachers find troublesome. Educational researchers have drawn attention to the relationship between disruptive behaviour among school children and difficulties with learning, especially of reading. For example, Lawrence, Steed and Young (1984) write,

> The precise relationships between educational problems and school behaviour are not always obvious but . . . . . the reading problem is often a primary factor. (p. 32)

They go on to draw a parallel between the growth of disruptive behaviour among school children and the increasing national crime rate. There is no doubt that there is much correlative evidence between delinquency and crime and the inability to read. This evidence gives us few clues as to cause and effect but the link is clear enough. Thompson (1991) suggests that,

> There is clear correlational evidence to link poor academic performance with problem behaviour. The findings generally show that behaviour disordered pupils have lower average IQs and are academically retarded in all areas. The evidence of lower IQ is not surprising considering the correlation between academic performance and IQ. What is not clear is the cause and effect relationship between the two factors. It is possible that a student who spends time misbehaving instead of working will fall behind in learning. The finding that student learning increases when teachers allocate a great deal of time to instruction while maintaining a high rate of task engagement lends some support to this view. The question left unanswered, however, is what factors may be responsible for the student's behaviour problem in the first place? Is it possible that a curriculum factor, i.e. the work was too hard, may have triggered the behaviour and the behaviour then prevented any progress toward remediating the academic deficit. (p. 54)

It is self-evident that the ability to read opens up a massive treasure house of knowledge, interest and delight. Having access to this provides the key to all kinds of activities and we all know how busy, interested people employ themselves; not, except for certain pathological cases, with crime and delinquency.

The particular concern of this book is not with the business of very young children learning to read, but rather with those who have made a start and then, for one reason or another, have failed to make good progress. Thus, bearing in mind the quotation above from *A Language for Life*, we shall not be very much concerned with the arguments between the protagonists of the various 'methods' of teaching reading. Nor shall we be bothered by conjecture as to what caused a particular child to fall behind. Instead, we shall be concerned with what can be done practically and immediately to remedy matters and start the child once again on the road to success in reading.

In its early stages, the business of learning to read is very labour intensive. It is necessary for the learner to have another person on hand who is able to overlook and read the text simultaneously in order to provide feedback about accuracy, general guidance and, above all, encouragement. There is an interesting parallel here with the even more difficult task which confronts the young child, that of learning language. It is intriguing to consider the fact that nobody seeks systematically to teach children to speak. They learn language chiefly from those in the family nearest to them and despite the sometimes poor and inconsistent model that is provided through everyday talk within the family, almost every child learns to speak. The teaching is carried out incidentally and by non-professionals, yet it is almost always successful.

Reading, on the other hand, is usually taught systematically by professionals and despite this a large minority fails to reach a satisfactory level, even after five, six or seven years of struggle. One important difference surely is that speech is instrumental. Speech enables youngsters to gain power over their environment, even at a distance. Words call for a response on the part of those nearby and children soon learn to appreciate the power of simple requests. Speech results in getting things done and making things happen, in getting goods and services provided. Later, children learn to use the word, 'No!' to good effect. Learning to read has no such immediate pay-off. In the early stages, reading brings about no prompt, instrumental effects in the way that speech does. It is only after considerable skill is being exercised in independent reading that it begins to pay off.

Having started on the road to reading the learner needs abundant practice. With spoken language he gets this all the time but with reading it is not necessarily so. *A Language for Life* included specific recommendations and among these was that,

> Every child should spend part of each day in reading or pre-reading activities. The teacher should give each child individual attention several times a week, helping him with his reading and keeping a meticulous check on progress. (Recommendation 85: p. 523)

Not too long ago we were regaled at regular intervals with data about the illiteracy of young men called up for National Service. Every now and again schools would be blamed for the fact that 18 year-olds could not read and write, yet this did not appear to have been the case when they left school. It was not that these young men could not read at all but that they did not read very well. In the opinion of those doing the testing, their ability to read was not functional and the reason, I feel sure, was that reading was rarely called for in their work and did not take up much of their leisure time. In other words, they were not getting enough practice.

This is a very important point. We learn to read by reading and we maintain our ability to read by practising; that is, by reading still more and all the time. Good readers interact with the text and will often offer spontaneous comments to teachers and parents in the course of their reading. In their search for meaning they are immediately aware when they have read something that does not make sense and they react at once by examining the immediate context. Good readers use the context (semantics) and their knowledge of how language works (syntax) to predict and anticipate. They check their predictions using grapho-phonic (letter/sound relationship) clues. Less confident readers ignore some of these strategies and have fewer ways of checking their understanding of what they have read. This is why it is so important for someone learning to read or someone who has fallen behind in their reading to have another person to read to. As soon as a child starts to sound out the letters of a word he or she loses the thread of meaning.

Let us consider how we, as skilled readers of the printed word, proceed when faced with a word that is unfamiliar. First, our rapid scanning of the text is interrupted as we encounter a previously unknown word. We search the context for clues because there is a very definite limit to the number of words which will fit into a meaningful context. Indeed, as we near the end of any sentence there are fewer and fewer words which can be used to complete it in a way that makes sense. If we have understood most of what we have read up to this point, we shall be able to make a pretty good guess as to the meaning of this new word and we shall probably be content to let it go at that, for the time being. Before long we may meet that word again, this time in another context. Having seen the word before we have a flying start in quickly sizing up the situation and will probably be able to interpret and understand three quarters of the meaning. On a further occasion we may encounter the same word again and then decide to look up the meaning in a dictionary, to find that our surmise was almost correct and that substantially we had worked out the meaning for ourselves. Surely, that is what skilled reading is all about.

What happens in many schools when teachers observe that children are failing to make good progress with their reading is that they are taken off reading and given something else to do. On the assumption that the task of reading is too difficult, teachers arrange for pupils to do something which is thought to be simpler, such as recognising particular letters or words. I can remember some years ago attending a course for helping slow readers in which we were encouraged to construct all sorts of games and other activities in order to help children recognise words. The assumption was that this was easier than deciphering text. The next assumption was that these words would be correctly recognised in context and that meaning would then become clear. I am sure that a great deal of time is wasted by this approach.

What is needed by pupils who are not making good progress in reading is the opportunity to practise and develop their reading skills; that is, their ability to cope with written words that are new to them and to gain meaning from text. It has been found that children who do not read very well tend to get *less* practice than those who are skilled readers. The reason is not far to seek. Nobody enjoys engaging in a task that is difficult and seems to involve failure all the time, so poor readers will try to avoid having to read. At the same time teachers find the task of listening to a reader who is struggling an onerous one. Between them teacher and pupil will, quite unwittingly, find all sorts of reasons for avoiding the reading task unless both display steely resolution. Above all, for success, the reading task must have some positive pay-off for the reader. We shall return to this point later.

Some writers suggest that self esteem is an important factor in learning to read and reference has already been made to the shame and lack of esteem felt by those who cannot read or do other similar basic tasks. We need to consider how self esteem develops. Ken Blanchard is an American psychologist working in the field of business management who wrote a book called *The One Minute Manager* in association with Spencer Johnson. Blanchard points out that 'People who produce good results feel good about themselves' and follows this up with a second aphorism that 'People who feel good about themselves produce good results'. Common sense tells us that feelings, effort and successful output are clearly linked. But then we have to ask what drives this association. Blanchard suggests that it is feedback. He says that, 'Feedback is the breakfast food of champions' and asks, 'How would an athlete training for an Olympic championship be able to improve if he did not receive feedback about his practice times?' Practice does not necessarily make perfect. It is practice with feedback that brings about improvement and that is why the early stages of learning to read are so labour intensive and why peer-tutoring can be so effective.

As already mentioned, children who are not making normal progress with the development of their skill in reading will fall further and further behind their fellows as the years pass. They need to make accelerated progress in order to catch up. The only way that they will achieve this is through practice at reading texts, chiefly narrative, that they can cope with and enjoy. They will thus learn by experience that to engage in reading is not a punishment but a real pleasure.

CHAPTER TWO

Why peer-tutoring?

If the conclusion reached at the end of chapter one is correct then teachers need to provide extra practice for readers who are making poor progress. How can this be accomplished?

Without going into the pros and cons of the various normative tests of reading ability it can easily be understood that when a child begins to read he or she needs to make steady progress in order to keep up with his or her peers. Once a child begins to fall behind whether through absence from school or lack of opportunity or encouragement he or she will soon begin to lose further ground unless some remediation is applied quite quickly. It is very easy for a teacher to miss the early stages of falling away and in many cases the problem will probably be observed only when it becomes quite serious. Then, as has been mentioned already, the child has to make accelerated progress in order to catch up with his or her fellows.

In the infant classroom teachers are already hard put to it to provide regular practice for every member of the class. Their time is limited and it is not uncommon for them to have two children reading aloud to them simultaneously. Thus, teachers find it difficult to hear those who are making good progress regularly enough. To arrange for the extended practice required by others who are not making satisfactory progress is even harder. Sometimes, parents are brought in to help with this problem and they can be very helpful. Parents of children who are having problems with their reading may be both willing and able to help by reading at home with their children but this calls for guidance from the teacher with regard to what books are most suitable and what procedures should be followed for the best results. Teachers cannot always give such guidance and this kind of information is what the present book seeks to provide. The procedures described here work just as well for parents as for peers as will become apparent from descriptions of some of the research.

Infant teachers are under a great deal of pressure to cope with the demands of the reading programme and tend to overlook the part children themselves can play if a scheme for peer-tutoring is adopted. This entails the tutoring of pupils by other children of the same age or slightly older (cross-age peers) whose own reading skill is more advanced by a year or two of reading age, as measured by a standardised test.

Few children who are having difficulty in keeping up with their peers in reading really enjoy the experience of having to read. They may be embarrassed to read aloud because they fear that their lack of skill will be shown up and that their mistakes will be criticised. Yet the need for them to do this is even greater than for those whose reading is satisfactory. Some children will need to be provided with additional incentives to engage in a task such as reading aloud that they find distasteful and even threatening, so it has to be made as attractive as possible with perhaps some extra pay-off for participating and further reward for any success that is achieved. Later on, when the child begins to realise that he can read for himself and that his skill is increasing, the intrinsic rewards of apparent success and the pleasure obtained from the story itself will be sufficient. But to begin with we have to be prepared to lean over backwards in order to get the process under way. This is one reason why contingent praise is such an important part of the more structured programmes like paired reading and pause, prompt and praise.

Firstly, however, we need to consider why peer tutors have proved to be so effective. (Accounts of some of the more formal evaluations of peer-tutoring schemes will be found in the chapters on research). Although parents are perhaps a more obvious resource for providing additional help they are not always available in sufficient numbers or at times which are convenient for the task. They may not be competent or prepared to be trained, or may not be available when the teacher needs to train them. Some parents believe that the formal teaching of their children is solely the responsibility of the school and that they should not participate or interfere. Of course, if parents are available and trainable they can do an excellent job.

Some parents are too involved personally with their child's problem to be effective as tutors. They may feel threatened by their child's failure and when they try to help find progress difficult and very slow. They become frustrated by this and think that they are somehow to blame. The resultant irritation may be vented upon the child and this is totally counter-productive: the child is put off wanting to read even more than before. Above all, parents do not know the most effective way to help and few teachers are able or willing to instruct them.

However, if parents are able to work with their own children and if, working together, they successfully remedy a weakness in reading the result can be an improvement in relationships all round. This was found to be the case in the Mangere Home School Project (see Chapter 5) carried out in Auckland, New Zealand by McNaughton, Glynn and Robinson (1981) after which several parents said the programme had led to a decided improvement in relationships between themselves and their sons. This was chiefly because the parents had been taught to use strategies which were clearly understood, carefully carried out and very successful in improving reading skills.

Secondly, peer tutors are plentiful and they are available for training at any time. Teachers can organise training sessions to suit their own convenience and to fit in with the rest of their time-table commitments. They can also make arrangements for appropriate monitoring of the tutoring procedures and of the progress made by the pupils, an important issue which was underlined in the Bullock Report (D.E.S., 1975).

Thirdly, it has been shown that readers who are making slow progress respond very readily to peer tutors. It has been suggested above that low-progress readers need extra help in embarking on a remedial programme that requires them to read aloud. What many slow readers lack is confidence in tackling the printed word and this is mainly because of their lack of progress thus far. If they are not sure how to pronounce a word correctly they will tend to hesitate or mumble. Anticipation of critical comment is likely to make them even more reluctant to try to pronounce an unfamiliar word and they will probably be prepared to accept, and even encourage, any help that is offered. That is why many low-progress readers tend to look away from the page when they encounter a difficulty and toward the person who is hearing them because they have learned that help is likely to come from that direction. This is a dependent behaviour which has been learned. Many people who try to help readers who are having difficulty (including some teachers) tend to supply the correct word as soon as a difficulty is encountered. This tends to encourage the behaviour referred to above which is a great hindrance to the development of independent reading behaviour which we are trying to develop. An independent reader would be looking at the text rather than at the helper.

To read to another child who has offered to help is totally different from reading to an adult, especially to a teacher. To have another child's assistance is probably going to be quite a novel procedure and the novelty itself may be sufficient to encourage a reluctant participant. It is probably less threatening and a less daunting prospect to read to another youngster, and every teacher knows that there are many occasions when a pupil will see another child's difficulty more clearly than they themselves. Working together engenders feelings of closeness and friendship and is good social training in itself.

Fourthly, there is plenty of evidence to indicate that by instructing someone else tutors will markedly improve their own skill in the subject concerned. In the words of the seventeenth century Czech scholar and teacher Comenius 'He who teaches learns'. There is no doubt that in the process of teaching someone else tutors improve their own skill in that subject. Indeed, one of the best ways of becoming master of a subject is to teach it to another person because, in the process of explaining it to someone else, you learn to understand the subject matter thoroughly.

In order to assist with the process of learning to read the tutor must come to understand the meaning of the words on the page and their relationships by considering them very carefully and the subsequent act of explaining or describing will further clarify them in his or her mind. This will occur during simultaneous reading, which is part of paired reading, and especially when deciding what has gone wrong in the pause, prompt and praise procedures in order to provide clues to help the tutee. (Both of these procedures will be described in detail later). Some parents may be heard to express the view that their children are in school to be taught and not to 'waste their time' as they might put it, teaching others. Fortunately, there are not many of these and some that are of this persuasion may be convinced if faced with arguments like those above.

However, helping somebody else learn to read does not only enable the tutor to improve his or her own reading. There are lots of other advantages to be gained at the same time and many rewards that are far from obvious. For example, tutoring is a very useful way of getting to know about the difficulties and problems facing other people and provides an opportunity for helping another person in a practical way. Teachers spend a great deal of their time attempting to inculcate social awareness and social caring skills. Tutoring provides practical experience and the opportunity to learn at first hand how to work closely with another person in a purposeful task. This is a far better way to learn about one's responsibility to others than a series of lessons in social awareness and moral values. It also gives the opportunity for the tutor to experience the personal satisfaction that comes from being able to help, and being appreciated as a result.

Some children known to engage in disruptive behaviour whilst having good reading skills have been given the chance to engage in peer-tutoring. As a result, by being given responsibility for a task that was seen to be useful and was approved of, they greatly improved their behaviour and their attitudes to school and learning generally. It is probably not too much to suggest that youngsters who have been involved in peer-tutoring of reading have learned a skill which will stand them in good stead later in life, not least when they have children of their own.

Until recently tutoring was seen primarily as a therapy; a means for the able to assist the less able. However, there is more to it even than this. It could well be argued that the opportunity to help someone else in their learning is a necessary part of every child's education. Tutoring would then be seen as something more than just an optional extra. Quite recently the Peer Research Laboratory at the City University of New York has been designing a new model to address the question, 'If the tutor role is so effective, why not build on this and give all students the opportunity to be a tutor?' The basic idea is to let the tutoring process become a central instructional strategy, integrated fully into every classroom instead of remaining a peripheral and remedial activity. Once this is accepted the approach may be viewed as developmental. Every child will have had the experience of being tutored before having the opportunity to become a tutor. It is suggested by those involved in developing this programme that much valuable learning is involved for both tutors and tutees. Initially, they will learn the subject matter, first by being tutored and then again and more thoroughly, by tutoring. Then, they will learn how to tutor, and how to listen and communicate effectively. Finally, and perhaps most importantly, they will learn about learning.

The people who are developing the scheme claim that this model:

a) calls for in-depth preparation and training of peer tutors and their outgoing reflection on the tutoring process;

b) removes the negativity usually associated with receiving help, since all students participate in giving and receiving help;

c) sees being a tutee as preparation for being a tutor;

d) leads to the creation of student-centred, peer-focused, schools.

Tutoring demonstrates openly and clearly the value of co-operation by giving tutors the chance to observe the difficulties of others and, by enabling both parties to get to know each other better, to learn the value of collaboration at first hand. The pattern of life for many of us is going to change in the future and will probably call for a far higher degree of collaboration and co-operation. It is likely that the need for such devices as job-sharing will increase in the future. The ability to be flexible and to work together with someone else may well prove to be at a high premium.

CHAPTER THREE

Setting up a peer-tutoring scheme for shared or relaxed reading

The first thing to decide is whether you want to organise a peer-tutoring scheme and for what purpose. Assuming that you have identified some pupils in your class who need help with their reading you will want to find out how many are involved and how far behind they are. This means using a reading test of some kind, preferably one that is administered individually because such tests enable a teacher to have a better understanding of a pupil's particular problems. Which one you use is not a critical matter so long as it is reasonably up-to-date and in common use because you will be interested in the scores mainly for the purpose of comparison, not as absolute measures of competence. (More information on appropriate test material is given in Chapter 11.) If you use reading scores at the outset and then at periods to gauge progress you must be careful not to use the same test again after too short an interval or the effects of practice will be seen and progress will appear to be greater than it really is.

You need to have a clear idea in your mind of exactly what you are trying to achieve in your peer tutoring scheme and how you are going to proceed. Is it a few individuals you are trying to work with? Are you working alone or are you responding to a school-wide effort to improve reading? Have you gained the interest of the children themselves and their parents? Who is going to be on hand to help with the organisation and running of the scheme: can you rely on help from other teachers or parents? Is there a Teachers' Centre or children's library to which you can turn for additional help? All these points are very important, especially if you are going to work with pupils other than those in your own class. Remember that it is usually easier to start with a small group and then enlarge the enterprise than to try to organise a large group from the outset. Working successfully with a smaller group also gives you confidence and assurance in your ability to organise on a larger scale.

Many teachers would think it invidious to single out particular pupils with problems and would prefer to involve the whole class or year group in a peer-tutoring scheme and, indeed, this makes some aspects of the project easier to arrange. If you are going to involve the whole group there is no need to consider what the rest are going to do whilst the scheme is operating and since the whole class will be engaged there is less chance that another activity will interfere with reading or that extra attention to reading will reduce the time allocated to other subjects.

Where the problem is seen as one of improving the general level of reading in the class and where there are no pupils so far behind that they desperately need to make accelerated progress the simplest form of peer-tutoring can take place. This has been called 'relaxed reading' by some people, 'reading in pairs' or 'shared reading' by others and 'paired reading' (incorrectly) by yet others. It means providing the opportunity for readers who need extra practice and extra help to read to someone else, usually on a one to one basis, for short periods at regular intervals. The teacher will need to give some assistance as to the books which will be suitable and even at this level some guidance needs to be given to the tutors as to the nature of the help expected. They should be asked to discuss the story with their tutees and to support, help and encourage them as much as possible. (See Chapter 7 on training for further detail.) Mutual enjoyment of the reading process should be the principal aim.

The essential element is that arrangements must be made for regular opportunities for tutoring to take place in circumstances which are conducive to progress, understanding and above all, to pleasurable enjoyment. The first and most important is a supply of books readily available, appropopriate to the skill level of the pupils, which will interest them and capture their imaginations. There is an abundance of such books today and details of what is available may be found from the information supplied in Chapter 12. Some of these sources may well be out of print but you will still find them in libraries. Most public libraries have a children's section and librarians with special knowledge of suitable books for all age ranges and such people are probably your best source of information and supply. Be prepared to get help from all available sources with regard to the supply of suitable books. Your own school library will be the first port of call but the local library will be prepared to help and Teachers' Centres may also have supplies of books to lend. There may be local advisers who are prepared to help with advice and information about where additional supplies of books are to be found.

In order to indicate which books are suitable for pupils of various abilities some form of coding may be necessary and for this a measure of readability may have to be used (see Harrison, 1980). Readability is a measure of the skill level needed to cope with the text. By applying a readability scale like the Flesch formula, for example, you can arrange the books according to their degree of difficulty. This takes time, however. Some series of books are arranged into levels already and an indication of difficulty in terms of reading age is given. Books obtained from school library services and from Teachers' Centres or Learning Support Centres are often already coded in some way to indicate level of readability.

Once the scheme is under way the pupils themselves can be asked to indicate the relative suitability of books by producing brief comments on those they have read. To insist that reluctant readers write a full report on every book they complete will tend to deter them from reading more, but to ask them to rate books on a few issues such as easy/hard to read, enjoyable/boring and so on should not prove to be too much of a chore. Whatever form of peer-tutoring you decide to set up be sure that you tell everybody who needs to know about it. The head teacher, your colleagues, parents and above all the pupils must know what you are trying to do, why and how. As well as knowing what is going on, you must be sure that they are supportive if your efforts are to be effective.

How will the pairings be arranged? If this is left to choice then some pupils will not find a partner and many may find themselves with unsuitable partners. Some judicious selection and persuasion will probably be needed to ensure that children needing help find themselves with a partner who is in a position to assist them. The tutor does not have to be very much ahead in reading skill, perhaps a year or so in reading age would be sufficient, although some authorities suggest that a difference of two years is best. If yours is a class with nobody too far behind then shared reading can take the form of reading together in pairs alternately, neither having permanent status as tutor or tutee. This has proved to be very popular and to work well.

If there are some pupils in your class who need extra help you may feel it necessary to pair them with other pupils who are skilful readers and therefore able to help more. More boys than girls are generally found to be behind with their reading. Many insist that boys are best tutored by boys and girls by girls but some recent research has indicated that boy/girl and girl/boy pairings work just as well as same sex pairings. Indeed, some boys preferred to be tutored by girls but this may have something to do with age.

If the whole school is participating in a peer-tutoring scheme it may be thought useful to use cross-age tutors, that is tutors who are older as well as being better readers. This has worked well in many schools but it may involve time-tabling problems. If it is school-based then the problem is reduced once a suitable time for everyone concerned has been agreed. Otherwise some complicated arrangements may have to be made to ensure that both tutors and tutees are available at the same time and this has resulted in some schemes being run out of normal lesson times; at break-times, lunch-times and so on. Such arrangements mean that the tutoring impinges on the pupils' own free time and this can cause problems. A child who does not find much enjoyment in reading will feel aggrieved at the prospect of losing his or her play-time unless there is some other obvious extra pay-off.

In some cases, however, it has been seen as a strength because only those who are really keen want to take part and motivation is a very important consideration in tutoring schemes. Pupils who are not interested in improving their reading will make poor tutees. However, the very novelty of peer-tutoring is often sufficient to encourage pupils to take part. Once they begin to make progress and find enjoyment in the process their motivation will become intrinsic, that is, from within. In at least one case, pupils from a separate secondary school have acted as tutors to pupils in a primary school, so ways of working around problems can be found if the motivation is strong enough (see Bamber, 1990).

If you are setting up a peer-tutoring scheme for the first time you may find it easier to begin with a small group rather than a whole class because organisational problems are likely to be fewer. Then, of course, if this is to take place within the classroom as part of the regular routine you have to think carefully about what the others will be doing. Reading needs to be done in a quiet and relaxed atmosphere which is not always easy to obtain in a classroom. This is yet another reason why peer-tutoring of reading often occurs outside the normal classroom time.

You may find that after a while your peer-tutoring scheme begins to run out of steam. Tutors, tutees or both may express the view that they are getting tired of the routine which, after all, can be quite demanding. According to the progress that has been made you might consider changing the procedure for a while. Both tutor and tutee might like to read together, but silently, and then spend some time discussing the passage at a convenient point in the story. Alternatively, you might decide to give peer tutoring a complete rest for a while and start up again after a reasonable break. The pairs might be changed at this point if thought desirable.

In any case, once a certain degree of skill has been reached, it is important to give pupils the opportunity to read silently, for this is the desired end product. Even when engaged in peer-tutoring to improve their reading skill children should always be encouraged to read other books on their own whenever possible. It has been found that silent reading in class is best achieved if the teacher also reads silently, providing a model for the pupils to copy. In most classrooms, when children are set to do a period of silent reading the teacher will engage in other tasks, perhaps hearing some of the readers who need extra help or doing managerial tasks like marking or preparing materials. It has been found that the modelling of reading by the teacher is a very important setting event for silent reading and that the amount of time the pupils spend reading is thereby increased. In some homes there are few books and reading is a pastime rarely engaged in. For some children to see an adult reading for enjoyment may be a very rare event indeed. To do so helps to dispel the idea that reading is something that is done only in school and only when instructed (see Wheldall and Entwistle, 1988).

Ideally, the opportunity for relaxed reading should be offered several times during the week but only for short periods of time; 15 to 20 minutes should be enough. The children taking part need to find themselves in a comfortable and quiet situation with appropriate seating. Tutor and tutee need to sit side by side so that both can share the text. Above all, they must be able to concentrate on their task in a situation that is free from interruption, noise and other distracting elements.

In addition to times when children are attempting to improve their own reading skills there should be occasions when children are read to. When the teacher is reading children may be introduced to texts which contain material which will interest and fascinate but which are too difficult for them to tackle on their own. They will not understand some passages but that does not matter. Where sections are thought by the teacher to be generally too difficult they can be omitted or can be followed by explanation and discussion. Whenever children are reading together or being read to, discussion of what has been read should be encouraged since it is by this means that understanding is improved and enjoyment enhanced.

Any scheme devised to improve the important skill of reading works best if it is part of a school-wide campaign to publicise and encourage literacy skills generally. This might include the organisation of book clubs; exhibitions of books and book covers (especially of new books); book, poetry and play readings; talks by experts on book writing and book publishing; play production and visits to plays and other productions; speaking and writing competitions and so on. Literacy skills flourish best in an atmosphere where such accomplishments are valued and nourished. Anything which can be done to interest and involve parents as well is to be encouraged. Children who come from homes where the parents are interested in books and reading seldom find themselves behind in reading, so if parents can be encouraged to take an interest in the efforts of the school to improve literacy they can play an important part.

Where pupils have reading deficits of more than a year or so it will probably be necessary to make arrangements for peer-tutoring to take a more structured form if progress is to be made. Here we may consider two such models 'Paired Reading' and 'Pause, Prompt and Praise'. The following chapters describe these in some detail. It must be emphasised at this point that all that has been said so far about frequency and duration of tutoring sessions and the need for comfort, quietness and freedom from interruption apply equally to these other forms of peer-tutoring.

CHAPTER FOUR

Paired reading

Paired reading was first described by Roger Morgan in 1976 in the journal *Child: care, health and development* and later by Morgan and Elizabeth Lyon in 'A preliminary report on a technique for parental tuition of reading-retarded children' in the *Journal of Child Psychology and Psychiatry* (Morgan and Lyon, 1979). Morgan reported that it was designed to meet two basic criteria. It had to be flexible enough to have general applicability with a capacity to adapt to individual (and changing) reading performance and it had to be simple enough to be used effectively by a child's own parents at home, with a minimum of training and supervision. In the beginning, therefore, paired reading was designed to be used by parents tutoring their own children.

The technique is said to be based upon behavioural learning theory in which reading difficulty is seen as lack of performance skill probably caused by a multiplicity of factors, about which no explanatory comment was attempted. The aim was to improve reading performance directly rather than attempting to improve underlying skills such as letter and word recognition. The method is one through which correct reading of continuous prose may be acquired through practice and in which the likelihood of success is increased through reinforcement. There are two basic components in this process: simultaneous reading and reading alone.

During simultaneous reading tutor and tutee read the text aloud and together, any adjustments in pace being made by the tutor. The tutee, whilst trying to read the page in front of him, is receiving visual stimuli from the printed page and auditory stimuli from hearing the other person read. Morgan describes this as 'participant modelling', in which the child is provided with a model of correct reading whilst trying to read for himself. The tutor is, in effect, providing a continuous prompt. While reading simultaneously the child is expected to pronounce all the words. If he fails the tutor signals this and allows time for a second attempt, modelling the word again if necessary. During this phase the reader is often successful in reading words which are unfamiliar by following the model provided and the suggestion is that such words may then be read spontaneously and without help on subsequent occasions.

Simultaneous reading may go on for some time, perhaps for many sessions, but when he feels ready the child may use a pre-arranged non-verbal signal to indicate that he wishes to be allowed to read on his own. A knock on the table or a gentle nudge is sufficient for the tutor to cease reading and allow the child to continue alone. Thus, the change from simultaneous to independent reading is under the control of the tutee. During independent reading the tutor gives frequent positive verbal reinforcement for correct reading, especially of spontaneously corrected errors and the correct reading of unfamiliar words recently encountered in simultaneous reading. The child is also praised for signalling because the aim is to maximise the proportion of reading done independently.

However, if the reader makes a mistake the tutor indicates that an error has occurred. If the child is unable to correct the error or read the word within four seconds the wanted word is supplied and repeated by the child. Simultaneous reading is then resumed until the child again signals a wish to read independently. The giving of immediate aid when difficulties arise is meant to avoid frustration and anxiety arising from non-productive effort and to ensure that the thread of the story is not lost. The reading material to be used is a text chosen by the reader and is, therefore, most likely to be of interest to him. It is suggested that provided the text is interesting and compatible with his chronological age the child will be able to cope, given the support at hand. However, it is essential to ensure that the text is not beyond the reading ability of the tutor.

The earlier paper by Morgan contained an account of his first attempt to use the techniques himself to tutor two boys and a girl who had reading problems. The tutoring was carried out at weekly intervals and the effects were believed to be positive but Morgan did not claim that the results were more than tentative. He suggested that more care was needed in training pupils in the method and that tutoring intervals and other matters needed attention. The later paper by Morgan and Lyon outlined the effects of an experiment in paired reading with four children tutored by their mothers. This time some of the points referred to earlier by Morgan were attended to and they were able to report considerable gains in reading skill by these low-progress readers.

The basic ideas underlying paired reading were developed by Keith Topping who was, at that time, an educational psychologist working for the Kirklees authority in Huddersfield. He encouraged its use in schools in the district and eventually set up the Paired Reading Project. This project produced a training video for paired reading and other support material in order to promote its use. Topping has published widely on the subject, being concerned especially with attempts to measure its effectiveness, and has been its staunch advocate over ensuing years.

The Paired Reading Project, in promoting the system, provides material to help teachers set up programmes and Topping suggests that the advantages of the technique are as follows:

a) Because they can choose the books they are to read children are allowed to pursue their own interests and, since they are given so much help, they can cope with books which alone they could not possibly read.

b) Readers are given the feeling of being in charge. They choose their own books and by giving the agreed signal they can choose when they want to have the opportunity to read alone. Failure is removed from the business of reading and this is very important for children who have been falling behind for some time.

c) The method is very flexible, allowing the amount of support provided to be varied according to the difficulty of the text, mood, degree of confidence and so on.

d) The responses of the tutor concentrate on the positive. Attention is paid mainly to the reader's success and this is probably in direct contrast to what has happened before.

e) The emphasis is upon understanding rather than the words themselves and that is what reading is all about. Through the process known as modelling, readers are given a good model to copy when they meet a new or strange word.

f) Simultaneous reading encourages continuity and flow. Where hesitation and failure predominate the text becomes fragmented and meaning is lost.

It is characteristic of poor readers that they read so slowly that they forget what they have read so far, thus losing the context and the meaning with it. Simultaneous reading allows the flow to be maintained and the context to remain intact so that pupils can use it to work out the meaning of new words. In addition, by listening to the tutor the child learns to pause and use emphasis appropriately, to give the proper pronunciation and inflection to particular words and thus to enhance the narrative.

g) Paired reading increases the amount of practice that pupils receive. They read frequently and they read quickly with the help that they are getting. Thus, they read more books, look at and decipher more words and so on. The effect of this is that they make clearly observable and measurable progress.

h) Paired reading gives a certain amount of structure to the process of learning to read so that each partner knows what to do and what to expect of the other person. In addition, the tutee gets the undivided attention of the tutor. Both tutor and tutee are involved in an enjoyable co-operative enterprise from which both benefit.

Thus, it is suggested that paired reading helps low-progress readers to increase their confidence in the reading process, to improve their understanding of what they have read and to increase their willingness to engage in reading as an activity.

The process of paired reading is best illustrated by using the diagram which appears on the next page. This may be used in order to teach the procedures and as an *aide mémoire* for tutors. The following points must be stressed in training tutors for paired reading.

In order to to ensure that the material to be read is interesting the tutee is allowed to choose the book, but it must not be too difficult for the tutor to read and understand. The pair should discuss the book before they begin to read. They can do this by looking at the title and the pictures together. It is suggested that opportunities for further discussion of the text should be seized as the story unfolds. The tutor and tutee then read together at the tutee's pace. Praise should be given by the tutor for correct reading but if the tutee makes an error of any kind the tutor is to carry out the correction procedure. The tutor says the word over which the tutee stumbled and may point to that word at the same time. The tutee repeats the word correctly and then they go on reading together.

The paired reading procedures

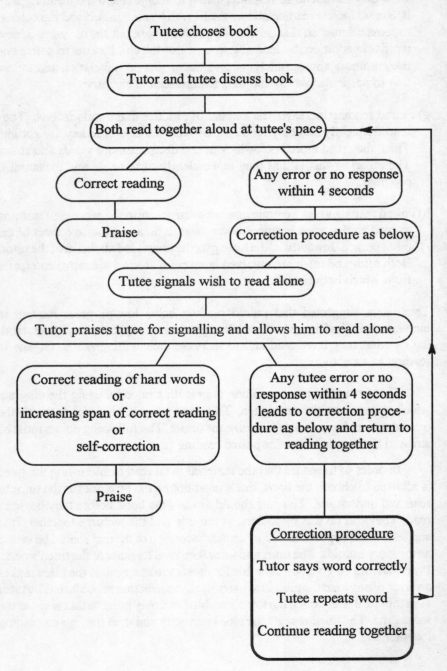

Tutee choses book

Tutor and tutee discuss book

Both read together aloud at tutee's pace

Correct reading

Any error or no response within 4 seconds

Praise

Correction procedure as below

Tutee signals wish to read alone

Tutor praises tutee for signalling and allows him to read alone

Correct reading of hard words
or
increasing span of correct reading
or
self-correction

Any tutee error or no response within 4 seconds leads to correction procedure as below and return to reading together

Praise

Correction procedure

Tutor says word correctly

Tutee repeats word

Continue reading together

When the tutee wants to read on his own he gives the agreed signal which may be a tap on the page of the book, a gentle nudge or similar sign. At this point the tutor would praise the tutee for signalling and stop reading. The tutee continues to read alone until he makes a mistake when the tutor applies the correction procedure, as before. Again, if the tutee gets stuck on a word he cannot read and pauses for more than four seconds the tutor applies the correction procedure. As soon as the correction procedure has been completed, simultaneous reading is resumed and the two read on together once more. It is suggested that praise should be generous and should recognise the correct reading of difficult words, an increased span of correct reading and, especially, when the tutee corrects himself, without being told, after having made an error.

It can readily be seen that some of the tasks to be carried out by the tutor call for maturity of understanding and of social conduct as well as expertise in reading. Choosing the book may be difficult without guidance from the teacher and discussion of it may cause problems for a tutor who has never seen the chosen book before. Reading together at the tutee's pace calls for some skill learning on the part of the tutor, whilst giving praise also calls for discretion and fine judgment, especially in such matters as an increase in the span of correct reading and the correct reading of hard words. Nevertheless, it has been shown that tutors can achieve these aims if they are carefully chosen and properly trained but it must be remembered that even adults, especially those who are not good and fluent readers, find some of them difficult.

CHAPTER FIVE

Pause, Prompt and Praise: its origins and development

The set of remedial reading strategies now known as pause, prompt and praise was developed within a research project carried out by Ted Glynn, Stuart McNaughton and Viviane Robinson whilst they were working at the Education Department of the University of Auckland in New Zealand. It was supported by a research grant from the New Zealand Child Health Research Foundation. The procedures were described first in their book, *Parents as Remedial Reading Tutors: issues for school and home* (McNaughton, Glynn and Robinson, 1981) which was subsequently published in England in 1987 under a new title, *Pause, Prompt and Praise: effective tutoring for remedial reading*. This later edition included a monograph by Glynn and McNaughton, first published in 1985, reporting a number of replications of the original study. The book reported details of the project which was carried out in a suburb (Mangere) of Auckland, New Zealand where housing was State financed.

The pause, prompt and praise procedures developed in this study later became the subject of a series of programmes which appeared on Pacific Television intended to bring them to the attention of the general public and to encourage their more general use. Permission was obtained at a later date for these programmes to become the basis for a training video produced by Wheldall, Glynn and Merrett and distributed by Positive Products. The New Zealand Council for Educational Research published a small booklet for parents called *Remedial Reading at Home: helping you to help your child* (Glynn, McNaughton, Robinson and Quinn, 1979) to accompany the programmes.

This project was strongly linked to the earlier reading research of Professor Marie Clay reported in her book *Reading: the patterning of complex behaviour* (Clay, 1979). Clay's 'Reading Recovery Project' which has recently aroused great interest in the U.K. was also developed from the same body of research. Basically, Clay argues that in learning to read children learn a number of quite complex strategies for predicting and working out unknown vocabulary. Learning to read is seen as a process of making mistakes (often referred to as reading errors or miscues) and gradually developing more efficient strategies using contextual cues, which relate to meaning and syntax, and graphical cues, which relate to the visual pattern of letters and words. As individuals learn to read they gradually learn to cope with reading material which is increasingly more difficult and so become *independent* readers.

The procedures which came to be known as pause, prompt and praise were developed by the researchers as the result of their interest in several related areas at that time. Having worked with Clay in the past they were interested to define proficient reading. They concluded that reading involves the use of two sources of information, the context, which depends upon language patterns, and meaning contained in words. They suggested that when the text is straightforward it is best to concentrate on contextual clues, using these to anticipate what is to come. When the text contains language or ideas unknown to the reader, graphic clues (such as, what does the word look like?) have to be used more. From consideration of their own research and that of others they concluded that the ability to discriminate different letter and word sounds accurately is, perhaps paradoxically, best achieved by concentrating attention on meaning and language patterns rather than on the letters and words themselves. Skilled readers have to become independent of outside help by learning to check for themselves the accuracy of what they have read in terms of, 'Does it make sense?' They also have to learn to self-correct any errors they make. Thus, skilled readers have learned to use a combination of strategies.

Glynn and his associates were interested in the importance of setting events, believing that behaviour can be changed by altering the conditions or environmental context in which it occurs. Of prime importance here is the level of difficulty of the text. If it is too easy it provides no challenge for improving skill. But if, on the other hand, it is too hard it leads to frustration, failure and loss of motivation. In order to progress, the reader needs to meet a succession of carefully graded books which get harder and harder but which never lead to frustration. Another important setting event is the general need for one-to-one instruction. Without individual tutoring the provision of contingent positive consequences and contingent feedback to errors is very difficult, if not impossible. Another important setting event is discussion of the story before reading begins. This provides an opportunity to anticipate probable events and outcomes and to preview unfamiliar words and concepts which are going to occur.

They believed that children are motivated chiefly by the consequences of their behaviour. Indeed, the power of positive consequences used contingently has been demonstrated widely in schools over many years through the use of tokens (ticks, stars and stamps), praise and other rewarding events. The important word in this sentence is contingently; for non-contingent rewards teach nothing of worth. Contingent consequences are those which are given, preferably quite soon, after the occurrence of an appropriate behaviour but *only* after that behaviour has occurred. Consequences then become entirely dependent upon the behaviour and thus will have their fullest effect. In a complex task like reading this probably means describing in some detail what was done that deserves rewarding like, 'You read that whole page by yourself. Well done!' The effective use of such positive reinforcement calls for a gradual shift in criteria. At the beginning a small success will call for a positive response but as skill increases only more complex behaviours should be rewarded.

Glynn, McNaughton and Robinson had already concluded that making mistakes is very important and is to be expected in the learning process. Children, like the rest of us, learn through making mistakes. Those learning to read quickly and successfully do this by themselves, because they soon become aware that what they have read does not make sense, but others, making slower progress, need help. Clay had already established that skill in self-correction is a characteristic of good, fluent reading. McNaughton and Glynn (1981) had researched the timing of feedback to oral reading errors and found that delayed attention to errors produced more self-corrections and an increase in reading accuracy, compared with immediate attention. Other studies had revealed that many teachers and most parents listening to children reading were likely to correct any errors immediately, without giving them a chance to realise that an error had occurred or to correct it. A paper has been published by Wheldall, Colmar, Wenban-Smith, Morgan and Quance (1992) describing how and how often this happens. Such a practice will obviously encourage dependent behaviour whereas the object is to develop independence in reading.

The Mangere Home and School Project

The Mangere project, having considered 14 families at the outset, was finally carried out with eight tutors (seven mothers and one aunt) working with eight boys, all of whom were several years behind in reading for various reasons. Generally speaking, the parents were concerned at the slow progress in reading being made by their boys in school but did not know how to help. It was decided that, to begin with, parents should be asked to help their children before being given any instructions. The purpose of this was to discover firstly, whether opportunities to read individually with an untrained adult would improve children's reading; secondly, to establish a baseline against which later changes in behaviour could be evaluated and thirdly, to determine whether the tutor-child interaction was actually as aversive as teachers were suggesting.

For the two older boys the Australian *Trend* series of books was used whilst for the younger boys the New Zealand Education Department's *Ready to Read* series was employed. Both of these are structured in levels of readability, having a number of different, short texts at each level to provide practice and allowing progress to be made to the longer and more difficult books in the series.

When parents were observed helping their children it was found that typically they intervened immediately rather than delaying attention to the child's errors, that they supplied the child with the correct word rather than giving prompts and that they used praise rarely, if at all. This tutor-child interaction pattern was seen as restricting children's opportunities for self-correction and for learning to correct errors with the aid of prompts. It was believed to foster their increased dependence on the tutor and thus to decrease their chances of becoming independent readers.

Each of the four researchers acted as trainer for two parent tutors. The procedures were explained and the parents were then asked to conduct a reading session using as many of the instructions as possible. During the session the researcher wrote down verbatim examples of both correct and incorrect applications of the tutoring procedures. For the first two sessions only, the researcher demonstrated several examples of correct tutoring following child errors. Immediately after the tutoring session, when the child had left, the trainer spent another few minutes with the tutor going over the verbatim examples. First the researcher prompted the tutor to recall what she had done when a given error occurred. For example:

Researcher: Remember when Alistair read 'Sally' instead of 'Susan'? What did you do then?

Positive feedback was given if the tutor remembered this accurately. For example:

Parent: Oh, yes, I said to him, 'Good, it's another girl's name. Look at the first part.'

Researcher: Yes that's right, you did exactly that.

If the parent could not recall the event the researcher would describe what happened using the verbatim notes. Having established correct recall of the particular event the researcher would next provide feedback on the effectiveness of the tutor's response. For example:

Researcher: You did well with that one. You praised Alistair for noticing that it was a girl's name and, since his error was already making sense, you gave him a prompt about the sound of the word. You said, 'Look how it starts' and Alistair then said, 'Susan'.

The researcher followed this up with a question and feedback on the tutor's response to this prompted correction. For example:

Researcher: Do you remember what you said when Alistair said, 'Susan' after your prompt?

Parent: Yes, I said, 'Good boy, that's right'.

Researcher: Yes, that's what my notes say too. You praised him for getting the word correct after you had given him a prompt.

Four or five examples were discussed in this way. Where the parent had responded in a manner inconsistent with the instructions, the researcher provided positive feedback for accuracy of recall and took the opportunity to ask, 'Yes, that's what you did. Now according to our diagram here what *should* you have done?'. The researcher then helped the tutor to locate the correct instruction on the diagram, before going on to the next example. You will have no difficulty in observing that the method being used to confirm correct responses and to draw attention to error bears a strong family resemblance to the pause, prompt and praise methods themselves.

For the first few weeks of the project researchers went along to the homes where tutoring was being conducted in order to help. All sessions were recorded so that even when they were not present the researchers could monitor these recordings to ensure that the procedures were being carried out correctly and to check on the progress being made by the boys.

A comparison was made between the behaviour of the parents before and after they had been trained to use the pause, prompt and praise procedures. The table below shows that the parents attended to roughly the same number of errors after being trained but that they responded to them quite differently. It is clear that after training parents delayed responding far more. They gave more prompts and more of these proved to be successful. Above all, they used praise far more than they did before they received training in the pause, prompt and praise procedures.

Condition	Errors attended to	Delay	Prompts	Prompts correct	Praise comments
Untrained	88.8 %	15.9 %	28.0 %	21.7 %	1.5
Trained	86.4 %	64.9 %	68.9 %	54.6 %	11.2

Table to show tutoring behaviour of parents before and after being trained to use the pause, prompt and praise procedures.

The progress of the children involved in this study was measured by observing their progress across book levels. When the boys were being tutored by their parents before training had taken place they certainly made some progress but this was increased greatly once the parents had learned and began to put the pause, prompt and praise procedures into use. The average number of book levels read to criterion during the month of untrained tutoring was 0.9 which is equivalent to about 1.5 months of progress in reading. The second phase of tutoring after the parents had been trained lasted two months but more than three book levels were attained during this period; an average gain of 6.5 months progress. This was accomplished with high levels of accuracy (87.3% words being read correctly) and of self-corrections (34.5% compared with 15% formerly). The writers suggested that,

The comparison of progress made under untrained and trained tutoring provides information on the importance of using specific tutoring skills, over and above simply increasing the opportunities for reading with a sympathetic and concerned (but untrained) familiar adult . . . When trained tutoring occurred, children read more difficult and longer books and, therefore, took more sessions to complete books. Nevertheless, the rate of book levels completed per month increased. (p.45)

As with paired reading, pause, prompt and praise started with parents tutoring their own children using the suggested procedures. However, in both cases attempts were soon made to involve others and, especially, other children in tutoring for the reasons already set out in Chapter 2. Many of these attempts were evaluated in a similar way to that adopted in the Mangere project and some of these will be described in Chapter 9.

CHAPTER SIX

Pause, Prompt and Praise: the procedures

Although these procedures are now known as pause, prompt and praise there is more to it than just pausing, prompting and praising. It is an approach which stresses that children learn to read by reading, not by learning a large number of separate words or sub-skills. It is essential that three important elements are supplied by the organiser of a reading project using pause, prompt and praise.

The first of these is the provision of reading material at an appropriate level. Here, the five per cent rule is very helpful. If a child makes fewer than four mistakes when reading a passage of fifty words then that text is appropriate for reading for pleasure. The success rate is such that the reading will be reasonably fast, meaning will be clear and interest maintained. If the pupil makes more than ten errors in reading a passage of similar length then it is far too hard and this is often referred to as frustration level for the reader. The child will be struggling to gain any meaning from the passage and will probably give up trying. Harrison (1980) refers to the fact that many children, even among those making satisfactory progress, find reading rather boring. He quotes one girl's comment as follows, 'If I start reading a book and come to a word that I can't read I think, "Oh, that book's too hard" and I just put it down.' The size of the print and the general appearance of the text can also be off-putting for the unskilful reader.

In order to ensure success we must provide reading material in which the child encounters some unfamiliar words but knows enough words to be able to make good predictions, even if some of these are errors. The right level of reading material can be broadly assessed by checking the child's rate of reading accuracy. If this rate is below 80% the text is too difficult whereas if the child is reading at over 95% accuracy it is clearly too easy. At a rate between 90% and 95% accuracy, promotion to the next level should be seriously considered. An ideal level for children learning to read, with all the advantages of making mistakes, is between 80% and 90% accuracy.

There is a simple and straightforward rule of thumb for ensuring that the text being read is at the most suitable level of difficulty. Listen to the child reading the first one hundred words in the piece and count the number of errors. From this the percentage accuracy may easily be calculated. If time is short the same calculation may be obtained from counting the errors from the first fifty words read and a decision can then be reached as to the suitability of the text. This is very similar to the five per cent rule mentioned above. Another way of assessing the relative difficulty of a piece of prose is to ask the child to place a finger on every word he cannot read and understand. If all five fingers have been placed on one page the text is too hard for that child.

The second element is that the child's progress should be carefully monitored with respect to the text, using running records and simple miscue analysis in order to identify particular difficulties so that they can be addressed and techniques improved. The reader may be found to have special weaknesses or display gaps in the skills necessary for decoding text. Some of the test materials mentioned in the chapter on evaluation may be very helpful in identifying weaknesses and suggesting further remediation programmes. Of course, when peer tutors are being employed, they cannot be expected to analyse errors. Detection and remediation of weaknesses in reading skill must remain with the teacher who will be able to gain knowledge of progress with errors and error correction from listening in or, better still, from audio-recordings made of the tutoring sessions. It may be possible, however, for tutors to note common errors made by their tutees to guide the teacher.

The third important requirement is that reading tutors should provide appropriate feedback as they listen to the child read. It is important to stress that mistakes (errors or miscues) are to be expected. Everyone learning to read will make mistakes. It is an important, indeed an essential, part of the process of learning to read. In other words, making mistakes is a good thing. By carefully monitoring the children's responses to text the teacher can readily work out if they are making average, or even better than average, progress and if they are using efficient predictive strategies. As has already been pointed out, Marie Clay (1979) suggested that children's rates of self-correction provide an index to progress in reading. Self-correction is seen as an indicator that children are reading actively in that they are able to 'solve' problem words independently. Similarly, we may recall that McNaughton and Glynn's

(1981) work showed that low progress readers, in particular, benefit from receiving feedback following an error.

Although the technique as a whole is now referred to as pause, prompt and praise; pausing, prompting and praising are involved in only the last of the three elements described above: that is the tutor's response to the reader. As was the case with paired reading, the procedures will now be described using the diagram on page 38 as a guide and *aide mémoire*.

Before beginning to read it is a good plan if tutor and tutee look through the book together so that the tutor can try to pick out any especially long or difficult words and anticipate unusual or unfamiliar situations. It is much easier to do this if the book is already familiar to the tutor or if the tutor has a chance to see the book beforehand. However, quite a lot of information about the content may be gained from looking at the title and the pictures contained within the book and talking about them.

Pausing

Once reading begins the tutor simply follows the text carefully until the reader either makes a mistake in pronouncing a word or stops reading. The tutor must then pause for at least five seconds or until the end of the sentence is reached, if that occurs before the five seconds are up. This gives the reader a reasonable opportunity either to correct his or her own error or to work out what the unknown word is, independently. Most reading tutors find that pausing is quite difficult but it is a key factor in responding helpfully to the child who is learning to read. To give the required word immediately is a very natural response of someone who is trying to be helpful. Indeed, they may believe that it is the best assistance that can be given but as research has shown it is, in fact, counter-productive. If readers are not given the chance to work things out for themselves they may develop habits, as described above, which make them too dependent upon outside aid and thus hinder the development of independent reading skills.

Prompting

If, after pausing for five seconds, no further response or another error is made, the tutor then gives a prompt. The type of feedback or prompt given will depend upon the nature of the miscue. If the child's error has not made sense then the prompt should be aimed at giving cues about the meaning of the word, by asking a question, perhaps. For example, if the child read 'hidding' instead

The Pause, Prompt and Praise procedures

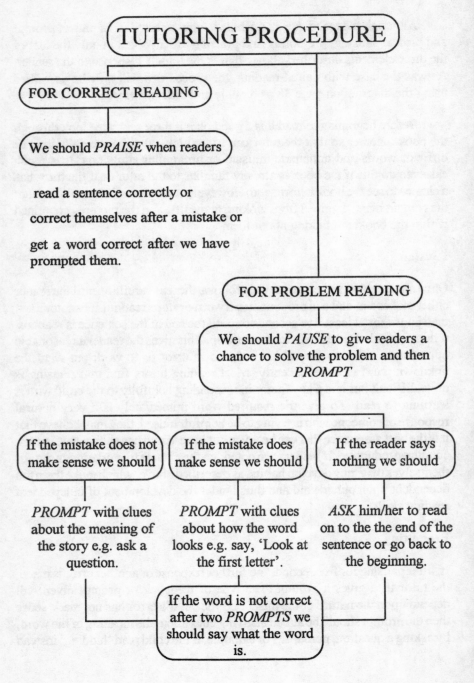

of 'hiding' one might say, 'The rabbit was trying not to be seen so what word would we use to describe him? He was . . . . . .?'

Sometimes the child's reading of a word, though incorrect, still makes sense within that context. In some cases one could maintain that there was no real error at all since the reading makes sense and the meaning is clear. Nevertheless, accuracy in reading is very important so the tutor's prompt should be aimed at helping the child to look again at the graphical properties of the word; that is, how it looks. For example, the child might read, 'The boat sailed out of the harbour' when the text actually was 'The ship sailed out of the harbour'. An appropriate prompt in such a case might be to ask the child to look at how the word begins. The child should then be able to see that a word beginning 'sh' cannot possibly be 'boat'. If he cannot do so, the indication is that he needs help in recognising some letter sounds.

Should the child hesitate and then say nothing, the tutor can (after pausing appropriately) either ask the child to read on to the end of the sentence or go back to the beginning. Often the context will help the child to work out what the unknown word is. In many cases a prompt is sufficient for children to determine the correct word but in instances where they are not able to, it is suggested that they are told the word after two unsuccessful prompts. This maintains the fluency of the story as far as possible and does not draw undue attention to the child's difficulty in responding correctly.

Praising

It is important to note that the praise should always take the form of a specific, descriptive comment. A comment like, 'Good boy' tells the reader very little. The positive feedback must be much more specific and indicate its contingent nature. For example, 'Good work, David. You corrected "rabbit" all by yourself' tells David exactly what he is being praised for and so the praise is clearly contingent upon good reading behaviour. This is much more likely to be effective, i.e. encouraging towards a certain class of behaviours such as trying to sort things out for yourself. In the same way a comment like, 'Well done Jean. You read a whole page by yourself, that's really good' indicates clearly what we are aiming for in good, independent reading.

Remembering and learning to carry out these procedures appears, at first sight, to be a complex business but it has been shown that with careful training and practice children are able to do so very competently. Training takes some time, however, and must not be skimped. Careful preparation of tutors will pay off in the long run. A sheet with the tutoring procedures on it, as on page 38, can be used as a prompt for the tutors to begin with but, with practice, they can soon be expected to carry out the procedures without it. Finding appropriate and effective prompts can be a challenge except for the brighter ones. Praising can also present problems for some. It is a good plan for tutors to be encouraged to compile lists of praise statements which they find effective so as to have a variety at their disposal. Part of the training should involve role playing in which tutors practise by tutoring each other before working with slower readers.

CHAPTER SEVEN

Training tutors and tutees

Whichever kind of peer-tutoring scheme you decide to set up it will be necessary to carry out some training with those who are to take part. You will need to meet the tutors to give them instructions, model the procedures and provide the opportunity for them to try out the strategies under guidance before attempting to work seriously with a partner. It will also be necessary to meet the tutees in order to reassure them about what is to happen and to explain the procedures. It may also be necessary to meet both together for some purposes. Whatever scheme you are going to adopt it is good practice to give both verbal and written instructions so that, apart from what they have heard, tutors have something to take away with them to look at after tutoring has begun to remind them of what they have been asked to do.

It is very important, at an early stage, to show all those who are going to take part what they are likely to gain from being part of the enterprise. For those who are going to receive help with their reading it will be necessary to provide them with reassurance that they will make progress and benefit greatly but that this will be a long-term process. As it is going to take time to show itself and since they are going to have to commit themselves to a lot of reading to achieve this some more immediate rewards must be built in. Some way must be found for them to receive positive reinforcement for carrying out their undertaking to engage regularly in a task, namely reading, that has given them very little reward and probably a great deal of grief, up to this point. This reward can come from you, the child's teacher, the school or the home or, best of all, from these sources combined. It must be something that appeals to the child, that is practically obtainable in a reasonably short time and it is best if it can be accompanied by some visible evidence like a chart or graph to illustrate progress towards its attainment.

With readers who are far behind it is especially important to arrange for the initial reading sessions to be short enough to be bearable and the rewards to be attainable in the very short term to begin with. Sessions can be lengthened by degrees and rewards made available in the longer term as progress is made and as the intrinsic motivation from success in reading takes over from the extrinsic rewards we are having to apply at the outset. It is rather like giving crutches to an injured person who is having to learn to walk again. They need the crutches to begin with but gradually they are able to do without. The whole process must be very gradual and preferably under the control of the learner.

In the same way the tutors who have volunteered to help need some additional incentive apart from their desire to assist someone who is less fortunate than themselves. Often children who have experienced some difficulty with their own reading in the past will be more inclined to lend a hand than some of the others but even these will need something to keep them going. In some schools they have been given badges or other form of recognition of their status. Certificates giving evidence of their contribution can be useful especially if these are included in records of achievement. Anything that can be found to recognise their helpful involvement and enhance their self-esteem is to be welcomed. Above all, their stint of helping should be kept reasonably short. Unwilling tutors are worse than useless. You can always lay them off for a while in order to recruit them again later. Girls have been found to be more likely than boys to offer their services as tutors so that particular problems arise in boys' schools in finding a sufficient number of tutors and keeping them. This is particularly trying since boys are, on the whole, more likely than girls to be behind with their reading.

Whichever model has been chosen tutors should be asked to sit alongside their partners whilst reading is in progress so that both can see the book clearly. Tutors should be responsible for keeping account of which book is being read, the pages completed at each tutoring session and any particular difficulties encountered. It is probably best if they are provided with a small notebook or card for this purpose which can be kept with the current reading book. If you are going to use paired reading or pause, prompt and praise you may have decided to tape-record all or some of the sessions. In which case, pupils will have to be shown how to operate the machines. It is necessary to have a special storage space for the books, notebooks, recorders, spare tapes and other equipment so that they are readily available when tutoring takes place. Pupils must be shown exactly where these things are to be stored after each session. This applies especially to the completed recordings so that the teacher can find them quickly and easily in order to listen to them. Tutors would also be expected to report to the teacher when a book has been completed to seek advice about what should be done next e.g. go on to a new book or begin a new book level.

If you are going to use relaxed reading (shared reading) then the instructions will be minimal. Tutors should be asked, once the pair are comfortably seated alongside each other so that both can see clearly, to talk about the title before reading begins and to encourage their partners to say what they think the story is going to be about. They should also look at the pictures and discuss what is going on, look at the names of the people involved in the story and any long or unusual words that may occur. Tutors should be asked to be as helpful and encouraging as possible to their partners. Such behaviours should be demonstrated by the teacher working with a volunteer so that they can understand what is meant. Tutors must be instructed not to be critical of tutees' attempts to make sense of the text as this is completely counter-productive and may lead to their giving up altogether.

If you are going to use paired reading, training is absolutely essential and a little more complicated. Teachers who are going to train others should first be expert in the method themselves and the best way to gain such expertise is to use the strategy for yourself. When we set up our training course in pause, prompt and praise for teachers we first taught them to use the procedures themselves and required them to carry out a programme with a child who had been making poor progress in reading. Only then did we work with them to set up training programmes for parents and peers.

As training individual pairs is very time-consuming, it is generally undertaken in a group situation. An essential component of this training will be a demonstration of the methods that are to be used followed by the opportunity to practise the skills since it is very easy to overestimate the effect of giving instructions, whether verbal or written. Good training implies both proper understanding, which involves clear instruction, and the opportunity for realistic practice.

A summarised outline for the paired reading procedures is given on page 26 and a copy of this should be used to tell pupils what they will have to do. They should be given a copy to keep by them whilst tutoring. The teacher should then demonstrate the two procedures, with a pupil as subject, while the tutors compare what is happening with their copy of the instructions. In order to maximise the effect of this demonstration the readability of the text used will have to be matched as closely as possible to the reading skill of the pupil. If the pupil can read the whole text without error the demonstration will lack credibility whereas if he or she can read very little it will be pointless. A training video may be obtained from the Paired Learning Project (see page 94).

Tutors then need to have the opportunity to practise the two strategies working with a partner, at this time probably another tutor. At all stages it will be necessary to stop and allow any who have not followed or who have a question to seek further guidance and it may be necessary to have a second training session. A final training period could then be held with both tutees and tutors present so that the teacher can observe how well the pairs are getting along and, perhaps, use the more successful pairs as models for the others. Just how long this will take and what will lead to the best outcomes will depend upon many factors and teachers will have to judge when the partners are ready to get on with tutoring by themselves. So as to avoid fatigue, training sessions should be no longer than 30 minutes.

Training for the use of the pause, prompt and praise techniques is likely to be a little more complicated than for the other methods of peer-tutoring because there are several procedures to be considered and learned. Nevertheless, it should be remembered that they have been taught successfully to all manner of adults and children, some with learning problems themselves. There is a training video in which the three feed-back procedures of pausing, prompting and praising are dealt with successively and this may be obtained from Positive Products (see page 94). (The paper by Houghton and Glynn (1993) describes how the components of pause, prompt and praise were introduced in succession over a period to some rather slow learners.) It will probably be as well to introduce and explain the three main strategies one by one. None of them is easy but the hardest of all for pupils is probably going to be prompting because this calls for understanding of the context of the reading error and the extent of the reader's language, that is, what they will be able to understand and what will help them best. Attempts to help with 'sounding out' the word should be discouraged.

Because the procedures are somewhat complex it is essential for teachers using this approach to keep a check on the performance of the tutors either by monitoring the reading sessions *in vivo* or by listening to a sample of recorded sessions. Unless the procedures are carried out properly and conscientiously we have no way of telling whether they are working or not. More details of how this may be done and how tutors may be coached to give a better performance may be found in Chapter 11 on evaluation.

CHAPTER EIGHT

The underlying research, Part one – shared reading and paired reading

In the next three chapters an attempt will be made to summarise some of the more interesting projects which have been undertaken to illustrate how effective peer tutoring has proved to be. There is no suggestion that this is a complete account of all that has been done but if you are interested in finding out more details of any of the studies mentioned you will find references to all those cited here listed in Chapter 12.

Note: in accordance with well-accepted practice children's reading ages will be reported as, for example, 8:4 which means eight years and four months. The colon indicates that months and years are meant and not decimal fractions of a year.

Research about shared reading

In 1980 Hewison and Tizard published a paper in which they identified a very important factor in children's reading attainment. This was the role that mothers played in hearing their children read to them. The study was carried out in two infant schools and a large number of factors was considered but,

> ... the factor which was found to be most strongly associated with reading success was whether or not the mother regularly heard the child read - not whether she read to the child but whether she heard the child read. (p. 211)

Two years later a second study was carried out (Tizard, Schofield and Hewison, 1982) in which children in two parallel top infant classes in each of two schools were compared. Children from one class in each school were given extra tuition in school and those from the other class were regularly heard to read at home. The tuition given in school was undertaken by experienced teachers specially appointed to do the job in consultation with the class teachers. They not only heard the children read but were concerned with all aspects of the teaching of reading. At school, children were seen in small groups but each child read to the reading teacher once or twice a week. Highly significant improvements were made by the children heard to read at home compared with those who received extra tuition in school.

In 1982 Bond wrote a paper describing how six persistent truants all about 15 years old were placed in a primary school where each was given the task of helping two children aged between 5 and 8, identified as slow learners. They were required to attend the school for eight sessions, each lasting two and a half hours. They accepted this responsibility, attended regularly and responded well to the younger children. The data were largely of an anecdotal nature but Bond reported that the tutors' attitudes to school and teachers all improved as did their self-concepts. Their own skills in reading and writing improved whilst the language and reading skills of the younger children were found to improve also. This is a well-documented account of pupils with behaviour problems improving after they have been given responsibility for tutoring but there are many others.

Wilson and Simmons (1989) found that even children with severe learning difficulties could be helped by tutoring but in this case the tutors were their parents. It is not beyond expectation that peer-tutoring could bring about similar improvements but great care would be needed in setting up the programme. A description of such a programme may be found in Chapter 9 (see Patch, 1993).

Atherley (1989) noted that poorer readers were largely wasting their time when they were supposed to be doing silent reading. The teacher, therefore, decided to carry out an experiment using peer-tutoring in the classroom. This was conducted with a class of primary school children who were well below their chronological age in reading and lasted for 12 weeks. During the programme the level of on-task behaviour rose considerably and more positive social behaviours were observed. Reading gains were considerable, the tutors making more progress than the tutees. However, Atherley claimed that,

> The most marked behavioural result was that the children's reading behaviour changed completely. When 'Shared Reading' was announced by the teacher, within two minutes the children had changed places into pairs - even choosing partners did not prove difficult - and only constructive activity ensued. All the children, not just the more competent readers,

became involved in the session and the time-wasting activities disappeared. (p. 150)

Thompson (1992) reported a study in which year 2 and year 3 children from a primary school were tutored by year 6 pupils. The children met in pairs with their leaders three times a week for 15 minutes at a designated time. Pupils with reading ages of less than 7 years were excluded from the scheme and given special individual help from their teachers at this time. The tutees did all the reading but were helped by the tutors to look for clues in the pictures or by help with phonics. At the end of the session the leader would test the reader for understanding. Parents were encouraged to hear their children read at home and it was believed that this made an important contribution to the success of the scheme. Over a five year period in which the scheme ran for eight months of the school year, the mean gain in reading was one year and six months which means that these readers were beginning to recover lost ground.

Swann (1992), finding that some 25% of pupils starting at a comprehensive school were virtually non-readers, set up a system of shared reading in which year 7 pupils were tutored by year 10 pupils, a cross-age scheme. After the first half-term of the school, when general assessments are made of literacy skills, all year 7 children are involved in peer-tutoring once a week for 15-20 minutes during registration period, each of the five forms taking a different day of the week. Each year 7 class has a year 10 class linked to it and five volunteers from this older group join them at this time. Pairing is largely voluntary, with some discreet direction from the teacher, but is not fixed. Some partners stick together, others change from time to time. The scheme is related to the literacy policy of the English department but the whole set-up is loose and informal because teachers do not wish to identify and label pupils who are having difficulty with reading. Of the 18 students taking part the majority made some progress in their reading and even more with their spelling. However, they barely kept up with their chronological ages and it is believed that one session per week was just not sufficient for them to make the necessary advance. The teacher writes of her greater satisfaction with the improvement in her pupils' attitudes to reading, their self-confidence and social skill, as shown in their completion of a questionnaire.

A different kind of organisation has been set up in a girls' secondary school where almost all the pupils are from ethnic minorities and most have additional difficulties with the English language. This way of working is made possible only because the senior management of the school recognise its vital importance and are prepared to make arrangements for it to work properly.

For several years now Uninterrupted Sustained Silent Reading (USSR) sessions (see Wheldall and Entwistle, 1988) have been held on two mornings a week for all pupils in years 7 and 8. This is part of a school-wide policy to encourage reading. Girls are encouraged to keep records of books they have read and to comment on those they like. Their recommendations are displayed from time to time for others to see.

During these silent reading periods pupils identified as needing help with their reading go to the library where they are tutored by girls from years 10 and 11 using a variant of paired reading. Many of the tutors (known as reading assistants) are bilingual and are able to use the mother tongue as well as English when working with their younger pupils. There is no shortage of pupils offering their services as reading assistants. In the Spring term, volunteers from year 9 are prepared for their role as reading assistants in preparation for taking over from year 11 pupils as the latter begin their GCSE examinations in the Summer term. This rolling programme of training and preparation ensures that the scheme has momentum and will go on from year to year. This is very important as girls will be entering this school for many years to come with the same language problems since many do not speak English at home. Some of the girls who were tutored in earlier years are now acting as reading assistants.

The position of reading assistant is regarded as a responsible one calling for real commitment and to acknowledge this the volunteers are awarded a coloured ribbon to wear which indicates their status and their particular language skills. Different coloured ribbons are awarded for different languages including Bengali, Punjabi/Urdu, Gujerati, English and so on. In September, 1993 there were 30 readers from year 7 and 26 from year 8 taking part with 34 and 30 reading assistants from years 11 and 10, respectively. There are more assistants than readers in order to provide for absence or other interruptions to the programme.

Both of these programmes have shown additional advantages apart from the improvement of reading skills for both tutors and tutees. Teachers report that the poorer readers improve in their confidence and interest in reading whilst the development of a sense of responsibility and concern on the part of the older pupils is thought to be very important. The system is believed to

Some interesting peer-tutoring projects have been set up in the Birmingham area. In a school for boys some pupils who had experienced difficulty with reading in the lower forms and who were now in year 10 were involved in tutoring those in year 7 who were currently experiencing difficulty. Time was found for this venture three times per week during assembly or registration periods. A good proportion of the tutees have made very satisfactory progress and, as a result, good relationships have developed between tutor and tutee. Good attendance is an essential for this progress and the very success of the scheme has brought with it some additional problems with the introduction of a second cohort, which calls for more space and more staff involvement. There are particular problems associated with setting up a peer-tutoring scheme in a boys' school. Generally speaking, boys are more likely than girls to be behind with their reading which means that a larger number of slow readers is likely to be found. At the same time, fewer boys than girls are likely to be interested in helping someone else in a task like reading. Sitting quietly and concentrating on the contents of a book is not the sort of pursuit that appeals to boys on the whole.

In the adjacent girls' school which taps the same catchment area, with a large proportion of pupils from ethnic minorities, a similar scheme has been set up but here the brighter pupils from year 10, mostly fluent readers, are involved as tutors. In both schools it has been found that about 20% of the annual intake need help with their reading if they are to make progress with their studies and these are identified through a screening process during the early days of the school year. Many of these pupils come from families where English is not much used in the home and, therefore, they have an additional language problem. In the girls' school partners more or less choose themselves and although they are free to change partners if they wish, rarely do so. In both schools the pause, prompt and praise procedures are used and serious attempts are made to provide incentives and rewards for tutors and tutees. For example, certificates are awarded which form part of the records of achievement for the pupils.

In both schools tutors are carefully trained and given written guidelines for what they have been asked to do. They are also given small notebooks for recording progress made by their partners. Teachers are on hand to listen in during the early stages to ensure that tutors are carrying out the procedures properly. In the girls' school tutors are given the power to grant commendations to their tutees, through the special needs teacher, when they do well or when they complete a book and these accrue towards the general reward scheme operating in the school. Both teachers operating these schemes try to involve the parents as far as possible by informing them of their child's involvement and of progress made. It is unfortunate that in the girls' school peer-tutoring can operate only once per week but despite this progress is quite evident. The scheme is so popular that some girls who have completed their first year in peer-tutoring want to go on. Unfortunately this is possible only for those who really need further on-going help. In both these schools staff members have become aware of the seriousness of the problem and are taking active steps to try to deal with it but there are many other schools throughout the country where the problem is not even recognised. Secondary teachers, generally, seem to be unaware of the fact that there is a high proportion of pupils who have reached the secondary stage without the ability to read

Bamber (1990) set up a peer-tutoring project in which third year girls from a secondary school tutored primary aged children who were having difficulty with reading. The programme lasted for six weeks and always took place at the same time every day namely, 9.30 to 10.00 a.m. This was accomplished despite the fact that the secondary school was a mile from the primary school. No formal evaluation of this project was carried out, the schools being more concerned with attitude change. They believed that both parties gained from the experience in many ways.

Following up the earlier work reported on page 45, Elliott and Hewison (1994) published a very interesting paper which described a study in which families from four different social backgrounds were compared to see what factors were likely to be influential in reading success. They found that reading success was strongly associated with the general level of literacy and the helping styles typical of the social groups observed. In middle class families emphasis was placed on the story content and meaning when hearing children read. In the working class and Asian families attention was centred more upon the mechanics of the reading process with help being given through phonics and the quick supply of words that were not read correctly. An interesting finding was that even though they lived in a rather poor catchment area from an economic standpoint, children in a group that had been involved in paired reading were, on average, able to read almost as fluently as children from the middle class group.

Research about paired reading

Keith Topping, working as an educational psychologist in Kirklees, developed the Paired Learning Project in the Huddersfield area of Yorkshire in the early eighties. This Project provides a range of services aimed at promoting achievement in basic skills by parental involvement and peer-tutoring and its function and effectiveness are now widely acknowledged. Many of the early studies were reported in the Paired Reading Bulletins published annually by the Project. Topping encouraged paired reading, at first in his local area, and then more widely and became associated with the Paired Reading Consortium which is still very active.

Topping and McKnight (1984) presented several studies using paired reading with parents acting as tutors. McKnight, working at Lydgate school, reported on three projects each working with 5 to 7 pupils and lasting between 7 and 8 weeks. The readers made improvements in their reading skill of between eight and 25 weeks in terms of accuracy and much more in comprehension. Ten other projects are reported, involving 379 pupils in all, where gains in reading accuracy were recorded of up to eight times the 'normal' rate. These are impressive improvements taking into account the fact that most of these children will have been making no progress at all previously and, indeed, may have been regressing.

In 1984 Winter and Low reported the Rossmere peer-tutor project in which 15 self-chosen pupils were tutored by volunteers from their own year group using the paired reading techniques. Tutors and tutees worked together for three 15 minute sessions three times a week for six weeks using level 7 or 8, as appropriate, from the Ginn 360 scheme. Tutees made average gains of six months and tutors did even better. Generally, children said that they preferred to be helped by other pupils rather than teachers or even their parents and all were keen to carry on with the scheme at the end of the period.

Limbrick, McNaughton and Glynn (1985) described a carefully control-led study in which three under-achieving 6 to 8 year-old pupils were tutored by three under-achieving 10 to 11 year-olds. Both tutors and tutees were selected randomly from two groups of low achievers in reading and they used paired reading, as originally described by Morgan and Lyon (1979), with two additional features, namely, delay in error correction and discussion of the passage before and after reading. Other pupils in the groups who were not chosen for the programme were used as control subjects. Gains for the tutees from between six and ten weeks of tutoring three times weekly were substantial. Reading ages were advanced by as much as six months. Improvements in their scores for reading accuracy were more than twice those of their control subjects whilst their gains for comprehension were four times as much. This study was able to show that most of the improvement in reading skill came as the result of applying the techniques of paired reading. To start with, tutoring had been spontaneous and undirected. Improvements were shown to occur *only* after training had been carried out and the techniques were being applied.

All the tutors also made substantial gains in reading ages for accuracy and comprehension over the course of the study. with the greatest gains occurring over the trained tutoring phase. (p. 949)

They concluded that, apart from arranging for pupils to help each other, it was necessary also to train tutors carefully in some procedures that were known to be effective. Simply to provide the opportunity for peer-tutoring was seen not to be enough on its own. The provision of a suitable structure and appropriate training for tutors was seen to be effective even with pupils who were underachieving. This is similar to the conclusion of Wheldall and Mettem's (1985) study to be described in the next chapter.

The fullest account, in a single paper, of studies in paired reading using peer tutors is to found in Topping (1987). Ten projects are fully described, all carried out in one local education authority. They took place in ordinary classrooms organised by teachers with no extra resources. Tutors were aged between eight and 18 years and tutees were from eight to 14. Necessarily, there was great variation in the kinds of training given to the tutors, the conditions under which the projects were carried out and the degree of rigour applied to checking procedures. In fact, very little attention was paid to these variables, mainly because the projects were organised and run by teachers who were doing this in addition to their regular jobs and not by researchers, who have time for this close attention to detail. The main focus was directed towards product or outcomes and the results were very encouraging. Topping claimed that, 'Both tutors and tutees gained in reading skill at approximately four times "normal" rates'. Since many slow readers are, in fact, falling further and further behind their peers without the help that peer-tutoring supplies this is a very worth-while outcome. Accelerated progress would allow them eventually to catch up, but even with continuing peer-tutoring the prognosis is not good. Very few projects have been reported which last long enough to bring about such a satisfactory outcome. Of course, this would depend upon how far behind the pupils were to begin with.

Greening and Spenceley (1987) suggested that paired reading is useful only for children with a basic knowledge of phonics and that the correction procedure involved in paired reading draws too much attention to mistakes. They also suggested that through being allowed free choice of books, some low-progress readers might find themselves faced with texts which were just too difficult for them and so suffer frustration when they try to read alone. They therefore adopted another model, which they called 'shared reading' which concentrates on the 'reading together' aspect of paired reading. Tutor and child read aloud together using a book selected by the child and all mistakes are ignored. The tutor's reading provides a model and continues even when the child is able to make little contribution on the assumption that the narrative is continued and interest maintained. The child can then resume reading when he or she feels able. Several projects were put in train using this method. In one of these eight 8 year-olds who were about two years behind in reading were tutored by this means for ten minutes on six days a week for eight weeks and showed a mean improvement of 11.6 months in reading age, using the Holborn test as a measure. A second study was carried out with infants and a third with 107 primary age children. Using the Salford reading test for pre- and post-project testing they were able to demonstrate mean gains of 6 months of reading age from a programme that lasted for eight weeks with ten minutes of tutoring six times a week. The third report was able to refer to improved attitudes to reading and to improved strategies for decoding text among those who had taken part.

Greening and Spenceley put forward the idea that their version of shared reading had a number of advantages over other forms. They suggested that, firstly, it was supportive for the child and very easy for tutors to apply. Secondly, in their study, it led to better relationships between children and their parents. Thirdly, shared reading, as they define it, is intermediate to being read to and reading independently and, therefore, has a very real place in the process of learning to read. Fourthly, the significance of phonic cues and of punctuation are learned naturally through the model provided by the tutor. They suggested also that attitudes to books and reading were improved as well as skill level. Finally, they claimed that whilst teachers would find the model easy to set up and to require little monitoring they would still be the organisers and motivators and remain in charge.

Miller (1987) attempted to discover which aspect of paired reading was the most significant in bringing about improvements in reading level. He was concerned to examine the quality of the 'reading together' phase and found that it was not very important. Pairs which appeared to be coping very well in terms of synchrony and so on were no more successful than those who found reading together much more troublesome. What did appear to be critical was the behaviour of both parties when an unknown word was encountered in independent reading. Where this problem was met with a four-second pause on the part of the tutor and a smooth return to simultaneous reading, success in improving reading accuracy was much more likely. He goes on to suggest that too much simultaneous reading may be detrimental and that the avoidance of attention to errors was the most difficult aspect of the method for parents. Here we see two quite different conclusions being reached by different researchers working at about the same time, yet both agree on the importance of having reading material which is appropriate and of the importance of pausing after a mistake has been made; matters which will be given further consideration in the next chapter.

Winter (1986) gives a useful summary of the paired reading procedures and describes some simple projects including the one at Rossmere reported above (Winter and Lowe, 1984). He was interested in examining the question of whether it is just extra practice involved which brings about improvement or whether the additional structure provided by the model being used had an additional effect. He concludes that paired reading has a decided advantage. He also gives a useful summary of advice for those about to set up a peer-tutoring project using paired reading.

Subsequently, Winter (1988) carried out a study in Hong Kong using paired reading with 10 and 11 year-old pupils in two primary schools. He found that the tutees made appreciable gains in their reading scores despite the fact that many of the tutors did not, in fact, carry out the procedures that they had been taught. He goes on to argue that the particular procedures used may be of little importance and that what brings about improvement is simply the fact the people are paying attention to the reading process and are generally stressing the importance of reading. This is at variance with his earlier study described above and some of the other studies where peer-tutoring carried out by untrained tutors has had little effect (see, for example, Wheldall and Mettem, 1985 and Limbrick, McNaughton and Glynn, 1985).

CHAPTER NINE

The underlying research, Part two - pause, prompt and praise

In the years immediately following the Mangere study, Glynn and McNaughton carried out a number of other studies using the same procedures and these were reported in Glynn and McNaughton (1985) which is included as a monograph within McNaughton, Glynn and Robinson (1987). The purpose of these studies was to provide a firm research basis for the procedures before promulgating them further.

> Replication serves two purposes: first, to establish the reliability of previous findings; and, second, to determine the generality of these findings under different conditions. (Hersen and Barlow, 1984, p. 325)

Glynn and McNaughton reviewed 11 studies which replicated the original experiment, with variations, carried out and reported in New Zealand, Australia and the United Kingdom. Including the original Mangere project the pause, prompt and praise studies had by this time involved a total of over one hundred tutors and 98 children between the ages of 7 and 12. Of these tutors, 62 were parents tutoring their own children, 31 were adults tutoring other children whilst 15 were older children tutoring younger ones. All the subject children had marked deficits in reading skills which varied from six months to as much as five years with a mean of about two years.

In eight of the studies comparisons were made between the performances of individual pupils before and after tutoring whilst three involved the comparison of groups of pupils. Some studies used progress through book levels to measure progress whilst others used standardised measures of reading achievement such as the *Neale Analysis of Reading Ability* (Neale, 1966).

One characteristic of pause, prompt and praise as set up in the original Mangere project was the monitoring of the tutors' and the children's responses by means of audiotapes. This is normally done before the training of the tutors to establish a baseline of skill performance for comparison. Invariably the levels of tutoring response have tended to be low e.g. for pausing less than 33%, for prompting less than 47% and, perhaps surprisingly, for praising (a much more natural and expected response) less than 8%. Typically these rates improved considerably with training which demonstrates that the procedures were readily learned by the tutors. The normal procedure is then to monitor maintenance of these behaviours through later examination of taped sessions. This was done in six of the replication studies and these gave firm evidence for the continued use of the learned strategies. Of course, the fact that the tutors were aware that some of their taped sessions would be examined later would be bound to have had some effect on these findings. Overall, it seems that the level of attention to errors did not change much. What did change was the difference in tutor response brought about by the pause, prompt and praise training and this would seem to be the critical element.

Six of the studies reviewed by Glynn and McNaughton involved parents tutoring their own children at home and in all of these the children made substantial gains in reading competence. Four of the studies were carried out in school only whilst in three the procedures were used both at home and at school. In the earliest study (the Mangere project) the substantial gains made by the children in reading at home did not generalise at all well to the school situation. This is difficult to understand until one appreciates that at the schools involved no opportunity was being given for the children to read appropriate and meaningful materials to their teachers. In the later studies, where measures were taken at home and at school, good evidence of appropriate generalisation was found since care was taken to ensure that children were given opportunities to read similar materials at school. The improvements in reading skill cannot be attributed simply to the tutor time given to the children as baseline measures relating to untrained tutoring have never shown any trend of improvement. Glynn and McNaughton concluded that,

> The consistent replication of treatment effects across the twelve studies adds to the growing confidence in the effectiveness of the original Mangere Home and School Remedial Reading Procedures. (p. 76)

Glynn spent some time in Birmingham in 1980-81 and whilst there carried out a study very similar to that at Mangere with parents of four 10 year-old boys in an inner city school (Glynn, 1985). The results were very similar to the New Zealand ones. All the children made good progress, the mean improvement in reading age after three months of tutoring being 6.25 months. The parents' tutoring behaviours changed markedly after training and as a result the boys' self-correction rate improved from a mean level of 12% to 25%.

Wheldall's early work with the pause, prompt and praise procedures which began in 1981, included three separate studies with both parents and peers (see Wheldall, Merrett and Colmar, 1986; 1987). The first of these was a pilot investigation of peer-tutoring carried out by one of his students. This small-scale study involved three groups of three 7 to 8 year-old children who were about six to 18 months behind in terms of reading age for accuracy. The peer tutors were six 10-11 year-old pupils from the same school of at least average reading ability. The results of this study were equivocal but it served as a valuable introduction to the rigours of this methodology and the practical problems of its implementation. What became clear, however, was that peers could be effectively trained to use all three components of the procedures.

One of the most thorough studies using pause, prompt and praise within a cross-age peer tutoring framework was that carried out by Wheldall and Mettem (1985). In this study eight 16 year-old low achieving pupils were trained to use the pause, prompt and praise techniques. The effectiveness of training such tutors was investigated through a programme in which these older pupils tutored eight 12 year-old remedial children who were on average three to four years behind in reading. The programme consisted of 24 tutorial sessions each lasting for 15 minutes over a period of eight weeks. Two matched groups of remedial readers were also monitored as control groups. One of these was tutored using the same periods and the same materials but by tutors who had not been trained. The second control group of eight pupils read silently during the same periods.

Since the tutoring periods were tape-recorded it was possible to carry out detailed analyses of the data reflecting what had been going on in the sessions. It was found that, unlike the tutors considered by Winter (1988), the tutors who had been trained did, in fact, carry out the procedures very faithfully. Comparing the two groups of tutors, one trained and one untrained, it was found that both paid attention to errors at a high rate, about 78%. However, whilst the trained tutors delayed attention to these errors at a mean level of 58%, the untrained tutors hardly ever did so (less than 1%). The untrained tutors hardly ever gave a prompt whereas trained tutors used prompts in 27% of their attention to errors and nearly half of these were successful. Again, untrained tutors hardly ever used praise. Trained tutors not only gave praise on average 8.8 times per tutoring session but they generally used their praise in specific ways, as they had been taught.

The result was that the pupils who had been taught by trained tutors gained six months in reading accuracy from their mean pre-test reading age of 8:4 years. The readers who had had untrained tutoring gained 2.4 months whilst those who had been reading silently gained 1.8 months. Considering that the programme lasted about two months the last group had actually lost ground. In addition, it was found that those who had been tutored by trained tutors had increased the number of self-corrections they made far more than had the other group. This, it will be remembered, is an indicator of growth in independent reading skill and is of prime importance.

The third of Wheldall's earlier studies, carried out with another of his students, evaluated a parent tutoring programme with young readers who were making good progress. Three groups, each of seven pupils aged from 5:6 to 7:6 with advanced reading ages were involved. One group comprised an untutored comparison group. Members of a second group were tutored by their parents who were given general tutoring advice whilst the third group were tutored by their parents who had been trained to use the pause, prompt and praise procedures. Pre-training (baseline) and post-training measures of parental tutoring behaviours were obtained from both tutored groups.

Briefly, the results again showed that tutors (this time parents) could be readily trained to use the pause, prompt and praise procedures. Before training, rates for pausing, prompting and praising were very low in both groups of parents but following instruction in the methods, the trained group paused after nearly 90% of hesitations or errors, prompted nearly 50% of the time (with 60% success) and used six times as much praise as before. The group of parents given advice of a general nature only, made very small gains in these skills. Interestingly enough, however, the results showed that for these young, skilled readers, tutoring using pause, prompt and praise led to no greater gains in reading than the general tutoring given by the other parents who had no training. Further replication studies carried out under Wheldall's supervision were reported in Wheldall, 1988.

From these preliminary studies researchers began to draw some tentative conclusions. It appeared that both parents and peers can be trained to use pause, prompt and praise procedures relatively quickly and easily. Where peers are involved there is much evidence to show that they, too, improve their reading skills. However, for children who are making reasonable progress highly structured peer-tutoring using paired reading or pause, prompt and praise is not really necessary. All they need is plenty of practice at reading material which is appropriate to their level of skill on a regular basis to a sympathetic listener. For older, low progress readers about to enter or already attending secondary school, however, it is a different matter. For pupils such as these, trained tutoring using pause, prompt and praise has been shown to be extremely effective and, indeed, very necessary.

On 25 March, 1986 a conference was held at the Centre for Child Study, University of Birmingham for teachers interested to learn more about the pause, prompt and praise procedures. It was attended by about forty teachers and advisers from all over the country. They were given information about the pause, prompt and praise procedures and informed about how successful they had been in the studies undertaken thus far. There was, of course, no time for training sessions although they were able to observe the training video. Most appeared to find the approach interesting and showed considerable enthusiasm to know more and to try out the procedures.

In the Autumn of 1986 Kevin Wheldall, Frank Merrett and Susan Colmar ran a course at the Centre for Child Study, University of Birmingham for a group of teachers under the auspices of the Department of Education and Science Regional Course Committee. The course was entitled 'Training parents and peers to use "pause, prompt and praise": a new procedure for helping older remedial readers'. Thirty three teachers enrolled for the course which ran for 10 weeks. The objectives were to teach teachers of older children (10-13 years) how to use the procedures themselves and then to help them set up programmes of their own using either peers or parents as tutors. During four of the early sessions we were fortunate enough to have Professor Ted Glynn, the leader of the original research team, with us.

As a direct result of the course, fourteen individual projects were set up, several teachers organising more than one (see Merrett, Wheldall and Colmar, 1987). Teachers were always entirely responsible for initiating and monitoring the projects which lasted from four to 23 weeks. Most of the tutoring periods lasted for 10-15 minutes and typically took place three times per week. Some of these projects were tutored by the teachers themselves, some by parents and some by older siblings. In six of the projects a standard reading test was used and gain in reading age was taken as a measure of progress. Such gains varied between two and 13 months giving ratio gains which varied from 0.9 to 4.7. (Ratio gains were calculated by dividing the gain in reading age in months by the length of the tutoring period, also in months.) In the other eight individual projects the organisers used book levels as a measure of progress and gains of between one and five book levels were made.

In addition to the individual projects some teachers were also able to organise programmes for groups of children with reading problems. Three such programmes were set up; two of them by groups of teachers and one by a teacher working alone. The largest of these had ten children, all but one of whom was tutored by another child. The other two had six and three subjects respectively and all were tutored by peers.

The largest of these group projects ran for 20 weeks with, typically, three sessions of ten minutes per week and produced gains in reading age of from three to 22 months (mean 11.9) and ratio gains of from one to 4.8 (mean 2.4). The group project with six subjects ran for seven weeks with five sessions per week each of 15 minutes. Gains varied from four to nine months of reading age (mean 6.7) and ratio gains of 2.3 to 5.1 (mean 3.8). The smaller group project with three subjects lasted for 12 weeks with three ten minute sessions per pupil per week. Gains in reading age were five, six and nine months and ratio gains were 1.7, 3 and 3 respectively (mean 2.2).

The children taking part in these projects were mainly between 9 and 12 years old. They were two, three or even four years behind in their reading skills despite a great deal of effort and energy having been spent by teachers over the preceding years. With almost all of them worthwhile gains in reading age or in book levels were made in the space of a few weeks of tutoring using the pause, prompt and praise procedures. For the first time most of them began to make progress at a rate fast enough to begin to catch up in their reading skills. The main objective was to encourage pupils' independent reading skills and it is believed that this holds out some hope for low-progress readers through peer and parent tutoring. Nevertheless, as with paired reading schemes reports of long term follow-up studies are rare.

In 1988 Yeomans reported a study carried out while she was teaching a group of infants using the Link Up reading scheme. Many of the children involved had learned, or were learning, English as a second language as they came from ethnic minority groups. The subjects for this intervention were the twenty poorest readers in their classes; the tutors came from a fourth year junior class and the tutees from a top infants class so this was a cross-age tutoring experiment. It was arranged for the better readers to tutor the better tutees so as to maintain the differentiation in reading skill. The children were placed in same-sex pairs and pairs were then allocated randomly to experimental and control groups, the former receiving pause, prompt and praise tutoring and the latter none. Fifteen minute peer-tutoring sessions were held three times a week for five weeks. The tutors, many of whom had generally poor levels of self-esteem, especially with regard to reading, were given badges to wear to enhance their status and these were highly prized.

Results indicated that the mean level of reading accuracy for the experimental group rose by 8.6% whilst that for the control group fell by 2%. Pupils in the experimental group increased the number of self-corrections by 8%. In the control group, where initial levels of self-correction were higher, the improvement was only 2%. Tutors from the experimental group gained six months in reading accuracy while the control group tutors gained only 1.4 months. Data collected from infant children before the intervention showed that many of them had been given texts from the reading scheme which were too difficult for them.

Wheldall, Colmar and Freeman (1991) trained community volunteers to use the pause, prompt and praise procedures with one group of six low-progress readers and compared them with another (control) group who were tutored by untrained community volunteers, who did little more than listen to the children reading. The pupils were from a metropolitan residential school which offers short term intensive remedial programmes for pupils with learning difficulties. Students taking part were roughly paired for reading age and then assigned randomly to the group taught by trained tutors or to the control group. Pupils in both groups received approximately the same number (about 30) daily tutoring sessions, each of about 15 minutes duration, spread over a period of seven weeks. Mean gains in accuracy as measured by the *Neale Analysis of Reading Ability* (Neale, 1988) were 13.5 months for the experimental group and 7.8 months for the control group.

Analyses of these data showed that the results for the experimental group were significantly higher than those for the other group. Similar differences were found for comprehension scores but these were not great enough to be statistically significant. Because of the unusual setting for this study, which was carried out within an already intense programme of remediation, the results cannot be generalised. Normally, in studies like this one, arrangements are made for tutees to have the same tutor throughout so that a relationship may be developed between them and this is believed to enhance the effectiveness of tutoring, but here it was not so. In this study, because of the way the community volunteers were employed, the students had a different tutor each day of the week but this did not prevent the tutoring strategy from being very effective.

More recently, other studies have been carried out in the Southern hemisphere by Houghton (Houghton and Bain, 1993 and Houghton and Glynn, 1993). In the first of these the subjects were eight 14 year-old below average readers who were trained to tutor eight students of similar age for whom English was a second language. Of the eight tutees, three were Yugoslavian and two were Vietnamese whilst the others were Indonesian, Rumanian and Malay/Chinese. The tutors were generally about four years behind with their reading and each was paired with a student of the same sex and roughly the same reading level. Each reading session was recorded and later analysed to see how successful the tutors had been in carrying out the procedures. Reading sessions were held daily for 20 minutes over a six week period whilst the other students were engaged in silent reading.

Examination of the recorded sessions showed that tutors had learned to carry out the procedures quite well and administration of the *Neale Analysis of Reading Ability* (Neale, 1966) before and after indicated that both tutors and tutees had improved their reading accuracy. The tutors gained an average of 8.2 months and the tutees a mean of 9.6 months in reading accuracy. For comprehension the average gains were 14.4 months and 13.7 months respectively and all these gains were significant statistically.

The pause, prompt and praise procedures might be thought by some teachers to be rather too complex for some pupils to learn. In his second study, Houghton sought to show that the procedures could be taught successively instead of all together. The participants in this study were all ten members of a class of below average readers withdrawn because of their problems in reading. Six of the group were boys and their mean age was 13:10 years. Each student was matched with a same-sex peer of approximately the same age and reading ability and the better reader in each pair was designated as tutor.

Reading sessions were held daily for 20 minutes during the time when other pupils were reading privately, the duration of the intervention being six weeks, on average. Pausing was introduced first and all the tutors managed to carry this out successfully. In successive weeks the two other procedures were introduced and were observed to be applied. As a result, tutees' reading accuracy improved by a mean value of 13.4 months and comprehension improved by a mean value of 14.6 months. For tutors the parallel improvements were 9.8 and 12.1 months. If teachers are doubtful about the ability of their pupils to learn all three procedures at once we have evidence from this study that they may be taught in succession with equal effect.

Henderson and Glynn (1986) looked at a very important aspect of the tutoring procedures, namely, the nature and style of feedback given to the tutors. They found that, just as parents' and teachers' interventions with readers tend to be immediate and very intrusive so also were the actions of most trainers when overseeing tutors at work. Four final year female teacher trainees taught the pause, prompt and praise techniques to parents who were tutoring their own children. The tutoring sessions were recorded and studied by the trainees. When asked to follow up these tutors and give feedback they tended to be very directive by telling parents where they had gone wrong and pointing out their mistakes very firmly.

Henderson and Glynn carried out their research in three stages to examine the effects first of parents' untrained tutoring, then of trained tutoring but with untrained students giving feedback and, finally, with the students having been trained to give feedback. They found that, as usual, parents who had not been trained hardly ever paused when hearing their children read, that they rarely gave prompts but told the child the correct word straight away and that they very rarely praised their child for good performance. Once they had been trained to use the pause, prompt and praise procedures they improved in all these aspects of tutoring reading but they became more expert still after the students had been trained to give feedback. The basic idea was to allow the parents to think about what they had done in a given situation and to solve their own problems, using similar techniques to those that they were using to teach their children to solve their own problems in reading.

The students were trained to discuss a situation with a parent in terms of what he or she remembered having happened or, better still, from a video recording. They might say, for example, 'What did Joan say for this word?' and then, 'What was your response?'. 'Yes, that was exactly the right thing to say but what happened when she stopped at this word? I can see that you recall now that you did not pause long enough.' The teacher trainees were encouraged to draw the attention of parents first to some instances where their responses had been correct and then to others where they had not been so successful in a way that would enable them to recognise and correct their own errors in the tutoring procedure. As a result the parents became much more efficient in their tutoring and their children made accelerated progress in reading. Examples of how similar strategies were put into effect in the original Mangere study may be found on page 32.

When presenting teachers with the 'pause, prompt and praise' procedures it has often been suggested that this may be good advice for parents or peers listening to children read but that, 'Of course, teachers do this already'. Subjective observations might cause one to doubt this glib assumption. Wheldall, Colmar, Wenban-Smith, Morgan and Quance (1992) reported a series of three studies which aimed to examine the truth of this claim. The first of these involved a sample of teachers listening to low-progress readers in upper junior, middle and lower secondary classes in mainstream schools in which 55 teachers were involved. The second studied 31 teachers listening to secondary aged pupils in special schools for children with moderate learning difficulties whilst the third looked at 55 teachers in junior/infant and first schools listening to children of average ability in the early stages of learning to read. In order to de-emphasise their role and to encourage natural responding teachers were told that the research was concerned with how children performed when reading aloud. Each teacher was asked to hear one pupil read on from where they had reached in their current reading book and to respond to these pupils in their usual manner.

Sessions were recorded and these were then analysed in a way similar to the evaluation procedures used in pause, prompt and praise experiments. Measures concerning accuracy and self-corrections made by the readers and the incidence of pausing, prompting and praising on the part of the teachers were all recorded. The level of reading accuracy was generally high and this suggested to the researchers that many of the readers were probably reading from texts which were too easy for them. It was found that teachers typically responded almost immediately to reader errors which meant that they allowed no time for pupils to self-correct. They were found to be most likely do this for the very low progress readers.

In other words, the slower the progress of the reader, the fewer opportunities to correct are provided by the teacher. (p. 190)

On the other hand teachers were quite good at giving successful prompts to their pupils. Praising, however, was very low in all three studies. A large number of the teachers hearing low-progress readers gave no praise at all whereas only 5% of teachers hearing regular readers gave no praise. It would appear, therefore, that this large group of trained teachers were little better than most parents at helping children learn to read. It is not surprising, therefore, to learn that parents seeking help from teachers in this matter seldom receive much useful advice.

It is believed that the issue of book level (raised above) is critical. If a child can read only three or four words from a ten word sentence there is little chance of him being able to utilise contextual cues, whereas if he knows eight or nine of the ten words his chances of predicting the unknown words are much higher, especially when given a contextual prompt. The implication of this is that book level is at least as important as the tutoring methodology; in fact, the effectiveness of the tutoring methods is contingent upon appropriate book level. Prompting, especially contextual prompting, will be much less effective where error rates are high.

Fear was expressed by some teachers and some teachers' organisations that by making strategies to improve reading available to peers and parents it would, in some way, devalue their professional position but this is quite unwarranted. Knowledge of paired reading or of pause, prompt and praise puts teachers in command of powerful strategies. Peers and parents can then be taught these effective tutoring skills by teachers. But it is the teachers who have to initiate, organise and guide, monitor progress, give advice about material and, finally, evaluate the outcomes. In all this teachers become managers of schemes which are too labour-intensive for them to carry out by themselves. They become instead, trainers, organisers and encouragers of others in schemes where good outcomes are highly desired, plain to see and almost certainly assured in the vast majority of cases.

Wheldall (1988) suggested that teachers should welcome the opportunity which peer-tutoring provides for non-professionals to be involved but should not allow the benefits to be thrown away by insufficient attention to detail. Apart from taking the initiative in publicising the approach and setting schemes in motion the teacher will be responsible for training tutors, for record keeping, for initial placement and subsequent promotion of children to appropriate book levels, for giving feedback on tutoring performance and so on. Parents and peers are extremely valuable resources for the effective tutoring of reading to low progress readers but the success or failure of any such tutoring programme will hinge upon the professional skills of teachers. This is where the skill of the teacher becomes paramount and his or her professionalism comes to the fore.

CHAPTER TEN

The underlying research, Part three - comparison and other studies

Several researchers have made attempts to compare different modes of peer-tutoring in order to see which is most effective. This is not an easy exercise because learning a skill is a very personal affair and the difficulties which people encounter are likely to be varied. In addition, it is difficult to measure the stage which a person has reached in their skill at reading and even harder, with the instruments that are available, to gauge any improvement. Lindsay, Evans and Jones (1985) compared two methods of tutoring namely, paired reading and relaxed reading (i.e. shared reading as defined earlier in this book). This was carried out with parents acting as tutors rather than peers. Twenty children aged between 8:7 and 10:4 years were involved. They were the poorest readers in their groups with mean levels of retardation of between 12 and 16 months. No significant advantages were found with either method and the researchers suggested that the simpler, relaxed reading was to be preferred as it was more cost effective.

Cusack (1993) also attempted to compare the effectiveness of paired reading and relaxed reading but used peers as tutors with children from a mainstream primary class. Thirty pupils aged between 7 and 8 were given the *Neale Analysis of Reading Ability* (Neale, 1988) and were divided into four groups according to their scores. Group A, the highest scorers were set to tutor group D, the lowest scorers, whilst group B, the second highest scorers, tutored group C. The pairs were selected randomly and assigned randomly to relaxed reading or paired reading procedures. Tutoring sessions were held on five days per week for approximately 20 minutes each day for twelve weeks which amounted to about 20 hours of reading time altogether. Unfortunately, despite the fact that the groups were allocated randomly, the two groups were not sufficiently homogeneous for the end results to be compared directly. The results indicated that both tutors and tutees in both groups improved significantly but, in this case, the poorer readers were not found to have done better than the others. From the way in which the study was organised there was some variation between the reading skill levels of tutors and tutees but examination of the results did not show this to be an important factor.

Leach and Siddall (1990) compared several strategies for helping children with their reading with parents acting as the tutors. Parents of 40 5 to 6 year-olds were instructed in four different methods of tutoring which meant that there were ten pairs in each group. The methods compared were shared reading, paired reading and pause, prompt and praise (as already described in this book) and Direct Instruction which is a much more controlled and structured method than the others, originating from the United States. Direct Instruction was described by the researchers as,

> . . . a comprehensive, task-analysed, phonic-based instructional programme which incorporates fully-scripted lessons and finely graded reading tasks based on a theory of instruction design . . . (pp. 349-350)

Steps were taken to ensure that the four sets of children involved had closely similar reading skills at the outset and that the amount of tutoring was the same, typically 10 to 15 minutes per week day for 10 weeks. Children were tested before and after the tutoring sessions using the *Neale Analysis of Reading Ability* (Neale, 1988). They found that there were significant differences in the progress made by the groups. Those receiving Direct Instruction made the most progress, followed by the paired reading group and the pause, prompt and praise group. Their conclusion was that,

> . . . increases in rates of reading progress can be expected if parents are taught more precise instructional methods that go beyond the provision of increased opportunities to practise, enhanced interest and reinforcement. In particular, there was a demonstration of the feasibility and value of brief training in Direct Instruction and paired reading techniques. (pp. 352-353)

What they failed to take into account was that pause, prompt and praise, especially, and paired reading to some extent, were intended not for beginning readers, as in this experiment, but for readers who were older than these children and who had fallen behind their peers in reading skill. Furthermore, there was no indication that those who were being tutored using pause, prompt and praise were given appropriate texts, which is a critical factor, as has already been explained. The authors suggest that pause, prompt and praise showed no advantage over shared reading in this study but they do admit that children so young could not derive the maximum advantage from pause, prompt and praise as they had had little time in which to develop reading strategies.

In the same year Diaper (1990) compared the two separate elements of paired reading i.e. simultaneous reading and independent reading with the standard way of carrying out paired reading, which involves alternating between the two, using parents as tutors. The intervention lasted for nine weeks with tutoring taking place for 15 minutes on six weekdays. The standard paired tutoring method proved to be superior to either of the other procedures alone and also to the results from a control group that had no tutoring at all. Gains were of the order of 7.4 'gains over normal' for the paired reading group as against 5 for the others. However, these rates of gain did not persist and had again fallen to 'normal' over the next few months. Diaper produced some evidence that the poorer readers gained most from all types of tutoring used in his study.

Patch (1993) carried out a study comparing the effectiveness of paired reading and pause, prompt and praise with a group of children who had been statemented as having special educational needs. As with most children of this kind one of their chief difficulties was with reading. Two groups, each of 15 pupils, were chosen from a group that were in a special unit for most of their time and all were at least two years behind in their reading. Their mean age was 14:2 years and their mean reading deficit was over 5 years. They were tutored at home by their parents using one of the methods for periods of between 8 and 10 weeks. The groups were tested before and after completion of the project using the *New Macmillan Reading Analysis* (Vincent and de la Mare, 1987). For the group who had received paired reading, tutoring gains were 10.6 months for accuracy and 22.8 months for comprehension and for the pause, prompt and praise group they were 16.5 months and 25.6 months, respectively. These results are highly significant statistically. Generally speaking, records showed that the parents using pause, prompt and praise had carried out the appropriate routines more efficiently than those asked to follow the paired reading model. This was also the case in a similar study by Osborne (1991) carried out in a mainstream primary school, where several pairs engaged in paired reading were lost because they did not stay the course.

Research about pairing

Foot and Barron (1990) carried out a study with 48 boys and 48 girls in which pairs were given a learning task (not reading) for which they were allocated to friend or non-friend pairs for one-to-one tutoring. Within each pair the roles of tutor or tutee were assigned randomly. Within the friendship pairs more interactions were observed but the results in test scores were not significantly different. It was concluded that friendship dyads appeared to impose extra burdens on children's limited resources through the need to negotiate new social relationships raised by the tutoring situation.

Topping and Whiteley (1993) carried out a meta-analysis on 15 peer-tutored paired reading projects carried out within seven schools in the North of England. The 186 tutees ranged in age from 7 to 12, as did the tutors, and projects generally involved the whole of naturally existing mixed-ability groups or classes. Matching of pairs wholly on a single-sex basis was carried out in only two of the fifteen projects, that is with 40 children. Projects varied in length and a variety of tests was used to measure outcomes but there were general similarities. The outcome was that gains for both tutors and tutees showed progress at well above 'normal' rates; over three times for tutees, on average, and even higher for tutors, as has been found quite often. Combinations of male tutors with male tutees did best in this analysis whereas female pairings while producing good outcomes for the tutees were much less successful for the tutors. Mixed-sex pairings were good for the tutors but poorer for the tutees especially for those with female tutors. It has to be remembered that in this study there were many uncontrolled variables to do with age differentials and choice. In one cross-age project, for example, mixed-sex pairings worked very well. Topping and Whiteley suggest that,

> . . . the robust effectiveness of male-male pairings is highly encouraging to those teachers who may often find it particularly difficult to motivate boys who are reluctant readers, especially if both tutor and tutee are low achievers in relation to chronological age. (p.66)

Topping and Whiteley drew attention to the fact that in the majority of studies relating to peer-tutoring pairings were of the same sex on the basic assumption that that would make for the best results. There is very little empirical evidence to show whether this is the case or not. A wide review of studies by Sharpley and Sharpley (1981) whilst reporting some studies which showed advantages for same-sex parings and others which did not concluded that,

. . . there is little support for the view that same-sex pairings are superior to opposite-sex dyads. There is also no support for the opposite contention. (pp.58-9)

Ainsborough (1994) set up an experimental study in order to examine the effects of sex pairing for pause, prompt and praise tutoring. The tutees were all from year 7 in a large mixed comprehensive school in the West Midlands of England. The tutors were year 10 pupils of the same school. She had four sets of dyads in which the tutees were matched for reading ability, as measured using the *New Macmillan Reading Analysis* (1987), allocated randomly to male-male, male-female, female-female and female-male pairing. All tutors were taught to use the pause, prompt and praise techniques and by means of recordings made of each tutoring session it was possible to ensure that the strategies were, in fact, carried out. This was a further demonstration that peers can be taught to use the pause, prompt and praise procedures effectively.

Pre- and post-project reading scores were compared and showed no significant differences between the groups. Same-sex and opposite-sex pairings had no observable effect and there was little evidence to indicate that single-sex pairings were any more beneficial to tutees than mixed-sex pairings. Whilst the sex of the tutor appeared to have no effect on the tutoring outcome some of the boys expressed an opinion that they would prefer to be tutored by a girl. Analysis of preferences arrived at through the completion of a questionnaire showed that tutees who had been allocated to a tutor of the sex they would have chosen, given the chance, did better than those whose choice was not fulfilled. Thus, it is possible that being able to choose one's tutor may be an important factor in the success of a peer-tutoring project.

Research on silent reading

Silent reading has always been a feature of school reading programmes and, in a sense, the ability to read silently is the end-product of learning to read. Wheldall and Entwistle (1988) set out to investigate the effectiveness of teacher modelling on the process of silent reading in class, following up some earlier work done in New Zealand. They carried out a series of studies in four upper primary classes and found that, in cases where the teacher sat down with the children to read a book at the same time that the pupils read theirs, performance was enhanced. In order to gain a measure of the reading activity they made careful observations using a modification of the OPTIC schedule (Merrett and Wheldall, 1986) which allows an observer to calculate for how much of their time the pupils are on-task i.e. actually reading. Normally, during silent reading sessions the children are asked to read whilst the teacher carries out other activities like marking books or hearing other children read and these tend to distract all but the most avid readers from their task to some extent. When the teacher is also engaged in reading for pleasure the whole situation changes and there tends to be almost complete silence and an atmosphere of concentration from everyone in the room.

In their experiments Wheldall and Entwistle manipulated the situation so that teachers first engaged their classes in silent reading while continuing to do chores and then adopted the Uninterrupted Sustained Silent Reading (USSR) ploy in which they, too, sat down to read. In some studies these phases were alternated and, whenever this was done, USSR showed higher levels of on-task behaviour, of from 10 to 20%, than in the standard silent reading lessons. It was not just that quieter conditions prevailed when the teacher was not listening to children read and that this brought about the improvement, however. This condition was compared with others where the teachers themselves were reading too and even higher levels of on-task behaviour were observed so it became clear that the teacher's reading behaviour was having an additional effect. There was some evidence to suggest that after periods of USSR, children were likely to spend their time more fruitfully in ordinary quiet reading sessions. Once classes have been taught to do this efficiently it provides an opportunity for the teacher to set up peer-tutoring projects for other children who have reading difficulties and this is what happens in a number of schools which have such schemes (see, for example, Swann, 1992 on page 47 and the descriptions of projects which immediately follow it).

In the same year Pluck (1988) reported a study carried out in New Zealand in which quiet reading times were manipulated in a similar way with a class of junior age children. To begin with the teacher would advise the pupils, 'It is reading time. Please read your own books quietly' whilst she went on with her usual classroom activities. After a while she began to model reading behaviour and would start the session by saying, 'It is reading time. I am going to sit here and read my book. It's really interesting and I'm enjoying reading it. Please read your own book quietly.' She would then concentrate on her own reading except if an emergency arose. During the course of the experiment these conditions were alternated and careful observations made of the children's on-task reading behaviour. Mean levels of on-task behaviour were shown to rise by 22% when modelling was in progress. Pluck comments,

Judging by the way some children in the present study stared and giggled upon seeing their teacher enjoy a book, this was obviously a novel experience. One wonders if some of these children had ever seen any adults, parents included, enjoy reading a book One also wonders if children not used to seeing adults modelling reading would be more or less inclined to imitate in the presence of their teacher modelling, than those children who come from homes where books are read regularly. (p. 112)

It may well be that some children are learning a lot more than is apparent from teachers modelling certain behaviours. It reminds one of the old saw about actions speaking louder than words and of the hidden curriculum which our own behaviour as teachers carries with it.

Yeomans (1992) carried out an experiment which showed that silent reading was possible even with children under the age of seven. She compared two styles of encouraging this process. One group of children received Smiley faces which were given to those who complied with the instructions which were to, 'Get on with reading your own book and stay in your place without talking to anyone else. Try to read your book in your head.' The rewards were given at the end of the ten minute reading session. For the other group good silent reading behaviour was modelled by older children who came into the room from another class. Both groups improved their ability to concentrate on reading to themselves but the second group who received modelling improved much more than the others. There was no difference between the results as between boys and girls. Lower ability readers made greater proportional gains in terms of time on-task but the difference was not significant.

Research which stresses social gains

Many of the research projects which have been described in this section have drawn attention to the fact that not only has peer-tutoring brought about changes in the academic skill of reading but has improved some aspects of the social context as well. Several of the school-wide studies have stressed this aspect as beneficial. In addition, some studies have actually concentrated on this aspect of peer-tutoring.

Franca (1983) carried out a study with the express purpose of finding out what would be the social effects of peer-tutoring. The children she worked with were in a middle school for those with behaviour difficulties. She set up a peer-tutoring project in which some pupils tutored others of the same age in mathematics. She used several different observational and other measurements and as a result was able to demonstrate that both tutors and tutees increased their success rates in mathematics. In addition, both improved in their attitudes towards the subject. This is to be expected since success in almost any endeavour is likely to bring about a change in attitude. In this experiment careful measurement of a number of social variables was undertaken and Franca showed clearly that there was a great increase in positive interaction between the members of the pairs as a result of the tutoring programme and a concomitant decrease in negative interactions as compared with the situation beforehand.

Limbrick, McNaughton and Glynn (1985) made a particular point about the improvement in social relationships which developed between the small number of tutors and tutees involved in their study. They related this to similar results when a whole class of children was involved in a subsequent study.

Houghton and Glynn (1993) commented on the fact that the tutors in their study all reported favourably on the programme. They consistently reported that they felt undervalued in the school and that the peer-tutoring programme gave them the opportunity to make a positive contribution which would benefit other students.

In conclusion, it may fairly be said that many aspects of peer-tutoring have now been thoroughly researched. The consensus appears to be that not only can peers be taught to use the various methods effectively but that these bring about good and positive results. In addition, there are many other benefits for teachers, peer tutors and the pupils who are being helped. We have to face the fact, however, that setting up peer-tutoring projects in schools is a difficult process. The hope is that teachers who read about other peoples' projects will be heartened by their success and that they will be helped by learning about how others have tackled the task.

CHAPTER ELEVEN

Evaluating your project

Human beings learn through experience but only if that experience is considered in terms of its outcomes. Despite the well-known aphorism that practice makes perfect we know that some people never seem to learn, no matter how often they encounter a particular problem. They always seem to make the same mistakes. In Chapter 1 the work of the American psychologist, Ken Blanchard, was mentioned and attention was drawn to his ideas about the importance of feedback. In order to obtain feedback about any new idea that we bring to our teaching we must engage in some kind of evaluation which usually involves measurement of some sort. If you have looked at the section on research in this book you will, no doubt, have observed the great care that researchers take to ensure that the outcomes of their projects are made clear and are, therefore, useful to other people. People engaged in research are keen to find out exactly what happened and why, so that they may learn from their work and carry it forward. Other people may want to try out what they have done and see if it works for them, too. This is what is meant by replication. This can only be done if the original research is very carefully described, measured in some way and then evaluated.

Most classroom teachers are not interested, indeed have not the time, to carry out research for the sake of it and are chiefly interested in outcomes with regard to the solution of their immediate problems. Even so, if we are to learn from any new enterprise we must be prepared to carry out some form of evaluation, however cursory. If you have spent time setting up a project intended to improve the reading of some of the pupils under your care you will, at the very least, want to have some measure of its success or failure. Otherwise you will not know whether all the effort you have put into it has been worthwhile and this will affect your willingness to go further with similar schemes. Even when you have adopted a procedure which has worked for others there is no guarantee that it will have worked for you and you need to know.

The production of some measure of improvement will be of great importance also in convincing others of the outcomes. It will be helpful in reassuring the children who have been involved that they have indeed benefited and improved their reading skills. Tutors will be interested to have evidence that all their hard work and dedication has had a good effect and that it has not been wasted. Some evidence involving a degree of measurement is much more likely to convince your colleagues of the value of peer-tutoring whilst parents will probably be more easily persuaded that what you have done has been worthwhile if some objective data can be produced.

What degree of rigour you apply to the evaluation of your work in peer-tutoring will depend upon your purpose in carrying it out and how much time and effort you are prepared to give to it. Clearly, if you have identified some children who are behind with their reading you will want to have some measure of their deficit before tackling any remediation. Not only will you want to know how far behind they are but also whether they have any particular problems and for this purpose will probably want to use a standardised individual reading test. Unfortunately, there is no reading test to date which enables one to evaluate a peer-tutoring scheme with precision because of the complex nature of the skill involved and the relatively brief period of training to which you will probably be restricted. The degree of precision with which we are at present able to measure reading ability is very limited and the time which you can give to teaching is also limited, even with the help of peer tutors.

The earliest reading tests produced by psychologists like Burt, Ballard and Schonell were, in fact, word recognition tests. They consist of lists of words of increasing difficulty arranged in groups relating to years of reading age. The child is asked to read the words and is then required to stop after a certain number have been omitted or mispronounced. These tests allow one to produce a precise score and a reading age in years and months related to norms obtained through the process of standardisation. Thus a child's ability to recognise certain common words is related to that of the average child in the sample that was used for standardisation purposes. In some cases these samples were very large and thus the tests were shown to be reasonably valid and reliable.

Unfortunately, these tests are now very old and out-of-date but even at the time of their first publication they were only fairly rough indicators of reading ability. They did not, in any way, provide an index to the child's understanding of what has been read. They related only to the recognition of words out of context; what used to be known as 'barking at print'. We know that reading is not only about being able to recognise words, in or out of context, but also about making sense of the printed page. It is as though a singer were to be judged by his or her ability to sing certain notes rather than to interpret a song. In addition, the reduction of a person's skill at such a complex task as reading to a single figure, suggests a bogus sense of accuracy and viability. Such a scale may be useful for placing the members of a group in order of ability but it can in no way be taken to give an absolute level of skill in reading, except for the rather sterile business of recognising words out of context.

Later reading tests attempted to measure the ability to read a piece of continuous prose with a view to gaining an insight into a child's ability to understand and interpret a simple story line. One of earliest of these was the *Neale Analysis of Reading Ability* first published by Macmillan in 1958, which has gone through at least two editions and many reprints. It has now been supplemented by the *New Macmillan Reading Analysis* (Vincent and de la Mare, 1987) which was developed along much the same lines. In both these tests the child is asked to read pieces of continuous prose in story form printed in an appropriate typeface with a picture alongside as might be found in a child's book. It is possible to gain three scores from the reading; one for accuracy by counting how many words the child reads correctly, one for speed by timing the reading of each passage, which are arranged in order of difficulty, and one for understanding from the answers to the questions which follow each piece.

In addition, the teacher has the opportunity to keep track of the mistakes made in terms of mispronunciations, substitutions, refusals, additions, omissions and reversals so that an analysis of the most common of these errors can be carried out. Before the child is asked to read the teacher is required to carry out an initial interview concerning the child's attitudes towards reading. Notes are made about the child's hearing and eyesight and during the reading session other aspects of the child's reading skill may be assessed by considering questions about the child's personal characteristics, word recognition and word attack skills, general reading habits and so on. Intelligent use of analyses like these produce a great deal of information and they have been used profitably in many of the studies referred to in the section on research. For children who read less well there is an alternative test, the *Individual Reading Analysis* (Vincent and de la Mare, 1990).

If you are going to use a standardised test like the Neale analysis for obtaining measures for planning and evaluating a peer-tutored reading scheme you will need to give the test more than once, for a before and after analysis. The trouble is that you cannot give the same test twice unless there is a fairly long time lapse in between or you will get a practice effect. It is pretty obvious that if a person has already taken the test once it will affect the outcome on the second occasion. They may make a better score simply because they are familiar with the test, its content and layout. The Neale analysis and its successor have three forms of the same test materials which are very similar and have been devised so as to be directly comparable. This means that a very similar test piece can be presented for reading within a relatively brief period.

However, serious doubts have been raised by some researchers about the comparability of these different forms of the same test, not without cause, so care needs to be observed. The cross-reliability of the three parallel forms has not proved to be very good so that many researchers using the Neale analysis, for instance, have tended to use the best of them (Form A) more than once provided that the testing times were not too close. Another snag is that the reading ages given in the table by which scores are converted are given in months and do not provide a fine enough mesh to show small gains in skill, even for reading accuracy. For comprehension, the situation is even worse because of the way in which this section is scored. In the *New Macmillan Analysis* a range, rather than a specific age, is given. This is much more realistic but makes it possible to recognise only very large improvements. The longer a project lasts, the more likely it is that some change will take place in reading skill and that this will be measurable but, unfortunately, for teachers there are many time constraints. Pupils move classes or schools and long term projects are difficult to set up.

The *Standard Reading Tests* devised by Daniels and Diack (1958) provide another means of obtaining reading ages and have been used in some studies. These consist of a number of sentences in the form of questions which the child reads and then answers orally. Children generally seem to assume that it is the answers to the questions that are important but it is, in fact, the reading that is crucial. From the score a reading age may be obtained or a reading standard (0 - VI). The level of discrimination is better than for many other tests and for evaluation purposes teachers may choose to use the raw scores since they are most likely to register change. The trouble is that this may be bogus and the result of chance factors. Daniels and Diack provide several other tests within their system which were devised for diagnostic purposes and these may be useful in helping some low progress readers. Unfortunately, their reading system is generally phonic based so does not ally itself readily to the peer-tutoring approach considered in this book, which is concerned with the reading of continuous prose for meaning and understanding. Nevertheless, the *Standard Reading Tests* could well be considered for evaluating a project.

Tests of reading ability like those already described are administered to pupils individually and this allows account to be taken of elements other than word recognition alone but it is time-consuming. There are other tests which have been constructed to be administered in a group situation. These are more useful for general screening purposes or for studies where the problems of the pupils are not so severe and the aim is to keep a general eye on progress.

If sets of data from two separate testings are to be compared it is very important that both are carried out by the same person and in similar circumstances paying attention to all the points in the instruction manual. Especially with poor and hesitant readers a test outcome can be greatly affected by a number of factors. The personality of the tester and whether he or she is known to the reader, the suitability of the room and the strangeness of the situation when the test is administered, the time of day and so on may all affect the outcome of the test. We must always be concerned to compare like with like and to ensure that, as far as possible, the situation in which the child is asked to read is 'normal'.

Another way of providing evidence of progress in reading skill may be provided by the use of a non-standardised test. Teachers may produce these themselves, buy them or obtain them from some teachers' centres. *The Real Reading Analysis,* which has only recently been published, is a good example of one of these. It is not difficult to produce such a test for oneself but it is rather time-consuming. What is needed is a number of pieces of continuous prose passages of comparable length, arranged in order of readability. These will probably best be related to the school's main reading scheme, if it uses one. Readability may be measured using formulae like those provided by Flesch, FOG or Mugford or by noun frequency counts as suggested by Elley. Descriptions of these and a full account of ways of measuring readability may be found in Harrison (1980). Readability may also be measured using the cloze procedure in which occasional words are deleted from text and have then to be reproduced by the reader from the context. Measurement using continuous prose passages will probably give as useful an index of progress as any of the other tests, but it will not be related to normative data.

A modern and thorough analysis of a child's reading ability may be obtained using *The Real Reading Analysis* (Bostock, Cooppan, O'Reilly, Perry and Swapp, 1990). It allows the teacher to carry out a full investigation into a child's reading difficulties including miscue analysis. However, this is not standardised like some of the other tests and does not give a numerical score or reading age. Nevertheless, it would provide a good index of progress made and would indicate some important areas where skill was improving.

Evaluation design

It is fairly obvious that when we are seeking to evaluate a scheme like peer-tutoring which runs over a time period we need to have some measurement of the state of affairs before it starts and another at the end. If it is to run over a long period we may well feel the need for some further measurement along the way to check on progress. Regardless of any teaching or other intervention from outside, the reading ability of a child must either be improving, regressing or remaining the same. One way in which we can check on this is to use a norm-referenced test over a time period and observe change.

Norm-referenced tests are those that have been standardised on many children from all over the country (preferably) so that a reading age of say, 7:4 means that the average child of seven years and four months would be reading at that level. All other things being equal we would expect that a child with a reading age of 7:4 at this moment would, one year later, have a reading age of about 8:4. This we might call a 'normal' rate of gain. Many of the children we would be concerned to have on a peer-tutoring programme would probably, as already mentioned, have been making slow progress, that is, slipping backwards over time. When we try to evaluate their progress we have to bear this in mind and relate whatever improvement they make to the 'normal' rate of progress because in order to catch up, these children have to make accelerated progress compared with everyone else.

The first thing then is to determine which test you are going to use and this may be decided as much by what you have to hand, how much time or money you can spare and how much assistance you have as by any other consideration. If you decide to use a normative test you will be able measure progress directly, allowing for the passage of time taken by your peer tutoring programme. If you are using prose reading passages you have devised for yourself you will need to compare the progress made by your tutees with that of some other children who are not currently receiving tutoring. In other words, you will need a comparison group. When researching new methods for helping with reading we need to compare experimental groups with others, called control groups, which are not receiving the same treatment, but the members of such groups should, ideally, be chosen randomly. This is so that statistical analyses carried out at a later stage may be relied upon as giving generalisable results.

For the purpose of comparing progress within a school it is quite sufficient to compare the tutored group with another (comparison) group so long as they are fairly similar in composition at the outset because it is very unlikely that you will be attempting any complex statistical analysis of the data. You may initially offer the tutoring to a group of 20 pupils but find that in the end only ten take part. The ten who drop out could be used as a comparison group but you would have to take into account the fact that those who opted out may be a special group. The very fact that they have not felt able to take part or that their parents have not been willing for them to be included means that they are different, in some degree, from those who are going to be involved. However, these issues are probably not of great importance for a school-based project.

As already mentioned, if you are using a standardised test you must ensure that it is given exactly as the manual instructs. Above all, you must on no account do any helping or coaching and, since you are probably going to give it more than once, you must ensure that the conditions are the same each time you use it. As far as possible, the place, the time and the person doing the testing should be the same for the reasons already given. With many of the tests you will probably find it easier to stick with the raw scores for purposes of comparison although with some groups, parents, for example, reading ages may be better understood. Generally speaking, a simple table will be sufficient to show the progress made. This example using raw scores is by way of illustration.

	Score at start	Score at end	Improvement
Pete	12	27	15
Steve	15	28	12
Mary	8	16	8
Sue	12	30	18
Gordon	13	24	11
Joanne	15	22	7
Means	12.5	20.7	8.2

On the other hand, if you use reading ages the table might look something like this one.

	Reading Age at start	Reading Age at end	Improvement	Subtract period of tutoring	Progress over 'normal'
Pete	5:6	6:0	6 mths	-2 mths	4 mths
Steve	5:7	6:0	5 mths	-2 mths	3 mths
Mary	5:4	5:6	2 mths	-2 mths	0 mths
Sue	5:6	6:1	7 mths	-2 mths	5 mths
Gordon	5:5	5:9	4 mths	-2 mths	2 mths
Joanne	5:7	5:11	4 mths	-2 mths	2 mths
Means	5:6	5:9	4.7 mths	-2 mths	2.7 mths

Again, if you use the Daniels and Diack reading standards your table might resemble the one below.

	Standard at start	Standard at end	Improvement
Pete	I	II	1 standard
Steve	I	II	1 standard
Mary	O	I	1 standard
Sue	I	III	2 standards
Gordon	I	II	1 standard
Joanne	I	II	1 standard

If you are using a series of books that is well structured with regard to book levels you could show progress by tabulating these levels in a similar way to that in the table above. If you are monitoring the progress of one or more pupils over a longer period of time you might like to draw a graph of progress at intervals which could be superimposed on the line of 'normal' progress. For an individual or group making rapid strides in catching up this could very encouraging whereas to someone who was far behind and making slow progress it would be very depressing and better avoided. An example of what such a graph might look like is given on the next page.

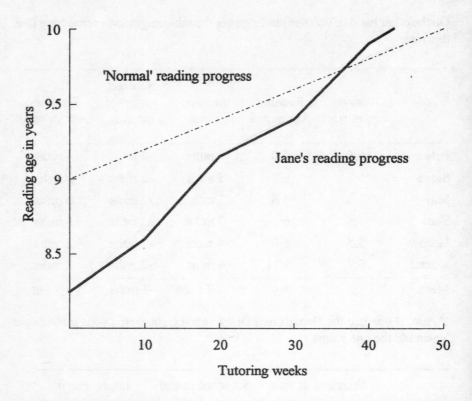

If you have adopted one of the structured schemes, like paired reading or pause, prompt and praise, apart from being able to measure the end product of your tutoring programme you will also be interested to see how far your tutors have been able to carry out the strategies you have taught them and how the tutees have responded. The best way to do this is to arrange for the tutoring sessions to be recorded on audiotape. Ideally, one would want to have recordings of all the sessions but this may not be possible. If you have to be selective try to do so on a random basis so that all pairs have an equal chance of being recorded. If you manage to have all sessions recorded you should then try to listen to a random sample of these. To listen to all of them would be far too time consuming for a class teacher, although we would probably try to do this in a full-time research project.

An attempt should be made to record what took place from this selected sample of recordings by using a check sheet like the one below. In order to do this you will need to have the recording to play back and a copy of the text from which the child was reading. You need to study this check sheet well, together with the following explanations. Under Reader Behaviour you will find a column headed, Word. In this column write each word from the text that was either read incorrectly or omitted by the reader. Under Response enter the reader's actual response for each of these words e.g. put 'went' if the correct word was 'want' or 'ele----' for 'elephant'. If the reader has omitted the word completely put a dash. Under Correction there are three possible entries. If the reader self-corrects an error without any help at all from the tutor put a tick under Self. If the reader corrects an error after being prompted by the tutor but without being told the word put a tick under Prompt. If the tutor has to tell the reader what the word is or if the tutor ignores the error put a dash in both Self and Prompt columns.

Under Tutor Behaviour you will find the column headed, Pause. Put a tick in this column if the tutor delays response to the reader's error. This indicates either that the tutor paused for at least four seconds or allowed the reader to carry on to the end of the sentence before making any response to the error.

There are four types of prompt which may be recorded and a column for each. Only the first two prompts used by the tutor should ticked. The four types of prompt are:

N - type prompt: this occurs when the tutor tells the reader that an error has been made but does not indicate what it is, e.g., 'No!', 'That's wrong!', 'Uh-uh!', 'Not quite', 'You've had that one before'.

R - type prompt: this is where the tutor gives an instruction either to read on past the error to the end of the sentence *or* to go back to the beginning and re-read the whole sentence containing the error.

L - type prompt: this is where the tutor provides the reader with clues about how the word looks or sounds, e.g. 'Sound it out', 'Look at the last letter' (or sound), 'Look at the first letter' (or sound), 'What does this letter say?', 'What do you think this part sounds like?' (pointing to part of the word), 'It sounds like your name'.

M - type prompt: this is the prompt where the tutor gives the reader clues about the meaning of the word in the context of the story, paragraph or sentence, e.g. 'Would that be "house" if it has ears and a tail?', 'Would that word be "boot" if it has seats in it and oars to row with?', 'How do you think father would drive if he had all the family in the car?', 'What happens to a boat when the engine stops working?'

PAUSE, PROMPT AND PRAISE: ORAL READING RECORD SHEET

	READER BEHAVIOUR			TUTOR BEHAVIOUR										
	RESPONSE	CORRECTION		PAUSE	PROMPT				Tell	PRAISE			
WORD		Self	Prompt	Delay	N	R	L	M	word	CA	SC	PC	O
1													
2													
3													
4													
5													
6													
7													
8													
9													
10													
Total													

A tick is placed in the 'Tell word' column if the tutor tells the reader the correct word either before or after giving a prompt. In addition, there are four types of praise comment to be recorded under their appropriate headings.

Praise - CA (praise for close attempt). This to be ticked if the tutor praises the reader for a close attempt or near miss, e.g. 'Good. That was nearly right but . . . . ', 'Yes, that word "ship" does make sense but look at the first letter (pointing to first letter "b")' or 'Great, you almost got it right'.

Praise - SC (praise for self-correction). Tick this column if the reader corrects an error without any help at all from the tutor, except for pausing, e.g. 'Well done. You noticed your mistake and put it right', 'Good, Sally, you figured that out on your own', 'Excellent, Tom, I didn't have to tell you that was wrong. You knew and said it correctly second time.'

Praise - PC (praise for prompted correction). This column is ticked if the reader uses a prompt and is then praised by the tutor, e.g. 'That's correct, Will. Now you've got it', 'You used that clue very well, Simon', 'That's it, well done! The word is "plenty" isn't it?'

Praise - O (other praise). Tick this column for any other (more general) form of praise not related to specific words or sentences, e.g. 'Your reading is coming on really well, Henry', 'I really like the way you read today, Susan', 'That was great, Amanda'.

Notice that this record sheet allows for only the first ten words that are read incorrectly. There is no need to go beyond this number. A thorough analysis of this sort would enable you to tabulate these data or draw graphs of them to see how well your tutors were managing. In addition, it would enable you to give tutors feedback on their performance in the way suggested by Henderson and Glynn (see page 63). It also gives you information about how well the tutees are faring because it gives an account of their progress and especially of self-corrections and these, as Clay suggested, are a good index to a reader's progress towards independent reading. However, you do not have to carry out such a thorough process of recording and analysis to enable you to keep account of what is going on. You can gain sufficient information about the tutoring to give feedback by going around whilst tutoring is in progress and making notes about what you hear and see. You need only to make notes of one or two instances of correct and incorrect responses on the part of your tutors to be able to give them some good feedback on how well they have been tutoring. If, in addition, you arrange for tutors to keep records of what happens in each session you will have quite a lot of information on how quickly books are being read, how soon tutees are passing from one book level to the next and so on.

Evaluation is bound to take time and effort. Setting up a peer-tutoring scheme is going to generate a lot of extra work anyway. What is the point of doing all that extra work and and then failing to find out what the outcome is? What is the point of effort, however worthy, unless you know how much has been achieved? It is surely worthwhile to attempt some evaluation, however rudimentary, to satisfy your need to know how things have worked out.

CHAPTER TWELVE

Sources of further information about peer-tutoring

Academic papers and chapters

Ainsborough, S. (1994). Gender pairings and the effectiveness of pause, prompt and praise. Unpublished M.Ed. dissertation, University of Birmingham.

Atherley, C.A. (1989). 'Shared Reading': an experiment in peer tutoring in the primary classroom. *Educational Studies, 15,* 145-153.

Bamber, S. (1990). Peer tutoring. *LINKS, 16,* 26-27.

Bond, J. (1982). Pupil tutoring: the educational conjuring trick. *Educational Review, 34,* 241-253.

Cusack, H.M. (1993). A comparative study of the efficiency of paired reading and relaxed reading using peers as tutors. Unpublished M.Ed. dissertation, University of Birmingham.

Diaper, G. (1990). A comparative study of paired reading techniques using parents as tutors to second year junior children. *Child Language Teaching and Therapy, 6,* 13-24.

Elliott, J.A. and Hewison, J. (1994). Comprehension and interest in home reading. *British Journal of Educational Psychology, 64,* 203-220.

Foot, H. and Barron, A.M. (1990). Friendship and task management in children's peer tutoring. *Educational Studies, 16,* 237-250.

Franca, V.M. (1983). Same age peer tutoring among behaviorally disordered middle school students: academic and social benefits to tutor and tutee. *Dissertation Abstracts International, 44,* 459.

Glynn, T. (1981). Behavioural research in remedial education: more power to the parents. In Wheldall, K. (Ed.) *The Behaviourist in the Classroom.* Birmingham: Educational Review Publications.

Glynn, T. (1985). Remedial reading at home. In Topping, K. and Wolfendale, S. (Eds) *Parental Involvement in Children's Reading.* London: Croom Helm.

Glynn, T and McNaughton, S. (1985). The Mangere Home and School Remedial Reading Procedures: continuing research on their effectiveness. *New Zealand Journal of Psychology, 14,* 66-77.

Greening, M. and Spenceley, J. (1987, April). Shared reading: support for inexperienced readers. *Educational Psychology in Practice, 31-37*

Henderson, W. and Glynn, T. (1986). A feedback procedure for teacher trainees working with parent tutors of reading. *Educational Psychology, 6,* 159-177.

Hewison, J and Tizard, J. (1980). Parental involvement and reading attainment. *British Journal of Educational Psychology, 50,* 209-215

Houghton, S. and Bain, A. (1993). Peer tutoring with E.S.L. and below-average readers. *Journal of Behavioral Education, 3,* 125-142.

Houghton, S. and Glynn, T. (1993). Peer tutoring of below average secondary school readers using pause, prompt and praise: the successive introduction of tutoring components. *Behaviour Change, 10,* 75-85.

Leach, D.J. and Siddall, S.W. (1990). Parental involvement in the teaching of reading: a comparison of hearing reading, paired reading, pause, prompt and praise and Direct Instruction methods. *British Journal of Educational Psychology, 60,* 349-355.

Limbrick, E., McNaughton, S. and Glynn, T. (1985) Reading gains for underachieving tutors and tutees in a cross-age tutoring programme. *Journal of Child Psychology and Psychiatry, 26,* 939-953.

Lindsay, G., Evans, A. and Jones, B. (1985). Paired reading versus relaxed reading: a comparison. *British Journal of Educational Psychology, 55,* 304-309.

McNaughton, S. and Glynn, T. (1981). Delayed versus immediate attention to oral reading errors. *Educational Psychology, 1,* 21-30.

Merrett, F. and Wheldall, K. (1986). Observing Pupils and Teachers In Classrooms (OPTIC): a behavioural observation schedule for use in schools. *Educational Psychology, 6,* 57-70.

Merrett, F., Wheldall, K. and Colmar, S. (1987). A 'pause, prompt and praise' course: new procedures for teachers concerned with children making slow progress in reading. *Behavioural Approaches with Children, 11,* 102-109.

Miller, A. (1987, April). Is there still a place for paired reading? *Educational Psychology in Practice, 38-43.*

Morgan, R.T.T. (1976). 'Paired reading' tuition: a preliminary report on a technique for cases of reading deficit. *Child: care, health and development, 2,* 13-28.

Morgan, R. and Lyon, E. (1979). 'Paired reading': a preliminary report on a technique for parental tuition of reading-retarded children. *Journal of Child Psychology and Psychiatry, 20,* 151-160.

Osborne, M.P. (1991). Teaching parents to use pause, prompt and praise and paired reading strategies at home: a study comparing the effectiveness of the two methods. Unpublished M.Ed. dissertation, University of Birmingham.

Patch, S. (1993). A comparison of paired reading and pause, prompt and praise: two programmes designed to improve the reading and comprehension levels of pupils protected by statements of special educational need, using parents as tutors. Unpublished M.Ed. dissertation, University of Birmingham.

Pluck, M-L. (1988). The effect of modelling by a classroom teacher on children's recreational reading. *Behavioural Approaches with Children, 12,* 103-113.

Sharpley, A.M. and Sharpley, C.F. (1981). Peer Tutoring: a review of the literature. *Collected Original Resources in Education, 5* (3), 7-C11.

Swann, D. (1992). Developing special needs provision in a Birmingham comprehensive school. Unpublished B.Phil. Ed. dissertation, University of Birmingham.

Thompson, I, (1991). An academic-educative approach to behaviour problems. *Positive Teaching, 2,* 51-64.

Thompson, P. (1992). Raising reading standards: the reader-leader scheme. *Support for Learning, 7,* 74-77.

Tizard, J., Schofield, W.N. and Hewison, J. (1982). Collaboration between teachers and parents in assisting children's reading. *British Journal of Educational Psychology, 52,* 1-15.

Topping, K. (1987). Peer Tutoring Paired Reading: outcome data from ten projects. *Educational Psychology, 7,* 133-135.

Topping, K. and McKnight, G. (1984). Paired reading and parent power. *Special Education - Forward Trends, 11,* (3), 12-15.

Topping, K. and Whiteley, M. (1993). Sex differences in the effective use of peer tutoring. *School Psychology International, 14,* 57-67.

Wheldall, K. (1988). Peer tutoring of low progress readers using 'pause. prompt and praise': further replication studies. *Behavioural Approaches with Children, 12,* 94-102.

Wheldall, K., Colmar, S. and Freeman, L. (1991). Employing community volunteers to tutor low-progress readers using the 'pause, prompt and praise' tutoring procedures. *Positive Teaching, 2,* 93-99.

Wheldall, K., Colmar, S., Wenban-Smith, J., Morgan, A. and Quance, B. (1992). Teacher-Child Oral Reading Interactions: how do teachers typically tutor? *Educational Psychology, 12,* 177-194.

Wheldall, K. and Entwistle, J. (1988). Back in the USSR: the effect of teacher modelling of silent reading on pupils' reading behaviour in the primary school classroom. *Educational Psychology, 8*, 51-66.

Wheldall, K., Merrett, F. and Colmar, S. (1986). Effective tutoring of low progress readers: pause, prompt and praise. *Behavioural Approaches with Children, 10*, 39-48.

Wheldall, K., Merrett, F. and Colmar, S. (1987). 'Pause, Prompt and Praise' for parents and peers: effective tutoring for low progress readers. *Support for Learning, 2*, (1), 5-12.

Wheldall, K. and Mettem, P. (1985). Behavioural peer tutoring: training 16 year-old tutors to employ the 'pause, prompt and praise' method with 12 year-old remedial readers. *Educational Psychology, 5*, 27-44.

Wilson, J. and Simmons, K. (1989). Right to read? Shared reading and children with severe learning difficulties. *Educational Psychology in Practice, 5*, 30-33.

Winter, S. (1985). Giving parents a choice: teaching paired reading and pause, prompt and praise strategies in a workshop setting. In Topping, K. and Wolfendale, S. (Eds) *Parental Involvement in Children's Reading*. Beckenham: Croom Helm.

Winter, S. (1986). Peers as paired reading tutors. *British Journal of Special Education, 13*, 103-106.

Winter, S. (1988). Paired Reading: a study of process and outcome. *Educational Psychology, 8*, 135-151.

Winter, S. and Low, A. (1984). The Rossmere peer tutor project. *Behavioural Approaches with Children, 8*, 62- 65

Yeomans, J. (1988). Pause, prompt and praise: a small scale peer tutoring project. *Behavioural Approaches with Children, 12*, 86-93.

Yeomans, J. (1992). Strategies for developing silent reading with infant children. Unpublished M.Ed dissertation, University of Birmingham.

Books about peer-tutoring schemes

Glynn, T., McNaughton, S., Robinson, V. and Quinn, M. (1979). *Remedial Reading at Home: helping you to help your child*. Wellington, N.Z.: N.Z.C.E.R.

McNaughton, S., Glynn, T. and Robinson, V. (1987). *Pause, Prompt and Praise: effective tutoring for remedial reading*. Birmingham: Positive Products. First published in 1981 as *Parents as Remedial Reading Tutors: issues for home and school*. Wellington, New Zealand: N.Z.C.E.R.

Topping, K. (1988). *The Peer Tutoring Handbook: promoting co-operative learning*. Beckenham: Croom Helm.

Topping, K. and Wolfendale, S. (Eds) (1985). *Parental Involvement in Children's Reading*. Beckenham: Croom Helm.

Other books referred to

Board of Education (1937). *Handbook of Suggestions for Teachers (The Pelham Report)*. London: H.M.S.O.

Blanchard, K. and Johnson, S. (1982). *The One Minute Manager*. Glasgow: Fontana/Collins.

Clay, M. (1979). *Reading: the patterning of complex behaviour. (second edition)*. Auckland, N.Z.: Heinemann Educational Books.

D.E.S. (1975). *A Language for Life (The Bullock Report)*. London: H.M.S.O.

Harrison, C. (1980). *Readability in the Classroom*. Cambridge: Cambridge University Press.

Hersen, D. H. and Barlow, M. (1984). *Single Case Experimental Design: Strategies for studying behavior change*. (2nd. edition) New York: Pergamon.

Lawrence, J., Steed, D. and Young, P. (1984). *Disruptive Children-Disruptive Schools*. London: Croom Helm.

Reading schemes with different levels

Ginn 360 series

Literacy Links

Longman Book Project

Longman Reading World

Skyways

Trend

Wellington Square

Tests and analyses of reading skill

Bostock, A., Cooppan, A., O'Reilly., Perry, L. and Swapp, J. (1990). *The Real Reading Analysis*. Wisbech: Learning Development Aids. (L.D.A., Duke Street, Wisbech, Cambs, PE13 2AE.)

Daniels, J.C. and Diack, H. (1958). *The Standard Reading Tests*. St. Albans: Hart-Davis.

Neale, M. D. (1966). *Neale Analysis of Reading Ability (Second edition)*. London: Macmillan.

Neale, M.D. (1988). *Neale Analysis of Reading Ability - Revised*. Hawthorn: Australian Council for Educational Research.

Vincent, D. and de la Mare, M. (1987). *New Macmillan Reading Analysis*. London: Macmillan.

Vincent, D. and de la Mare, M. (1990). *Individual Reading Analysis: Teachers' Guide*. Slough: NFER-Nelson.

A copy of their catalogue of reading and other tests may be obtained by writing to NFER-Nelson, Darville House, 2 Oxford Road East, Windsor, Berkshire, SL4 1DF.

Information about reading books for children

Barnicoats, Parkengue, Penryn, Cornwall, TR10 9EP.

Carpenter, H. *Secret Gardens: the golden age of children's literature*. London: Unwin.

Fisher, M. (1964). *Intent Upon Reading*. Leicester: Brockhampton Press.

Fisher, M. *Classics for Children and Young People*. (May be obtained from The Thimble Press: see below for address.)

Random House Children's Books, 20 Vauxhall Bridge Road, London, SW1V 2SA.

Signal: Approaches to Children's Books is published three times a year by the Thimble Press, Lockwood, Station Road, South Woodchester, Stroud, Gloucestershire, GL5 5EQ.

Townsend, J.R. (1965). *Written for Children*. Harmondsworth: Penguin.

Associations concerned about reading and reading standards

Federation of Children's Book Groups, (Madeleine Rubach), The Blue House, 10 Cook Road, Aldbourne, Marlborough, Wiltshire SN8 2EG.

Librarians of Institutes and Schools of Education, Publications, (Frances Wood, B.A., A.L.A.) Education Library, University College Swansea, Gower Road, Hendrefoilan, Swansea, SA5 7NB.

The National Association for Special Educational Needs, 2 Lichfield Road, Stafford, ST17 4JX.

School Library Association, Liden Library, Barrington Close, Liden, Swindon, Wiltshire, SN3 6HF.

Society of County Children's and Education Librarians, (Hon. Sec., Catherine Blanshard, A.L.A.), Libraries, Arts and Information, New Barnfield, Travellers' Lane, Hatfield, AL10 8XG.

Useful information about their current lists of titles and of future publications may be obtained by writing to any of these organisations.

Other sources of information

Information about the Pause, Prompt and Praise technique may be obtained from Dr Frank Merrett, c/o Positive Products, P.O. Box 45, Cheltenham, Glos., GL52 3BX. Tel: 0242 233227.

The Paired Reading Training Pack and the Paired Reading Bulletins are available from: The Paired Learning Project, Kirklees Psychological Service, Oldgate House, 2 Oldgate, Huddersfield, HD1 6QW. Tel: 0484 537399

Index